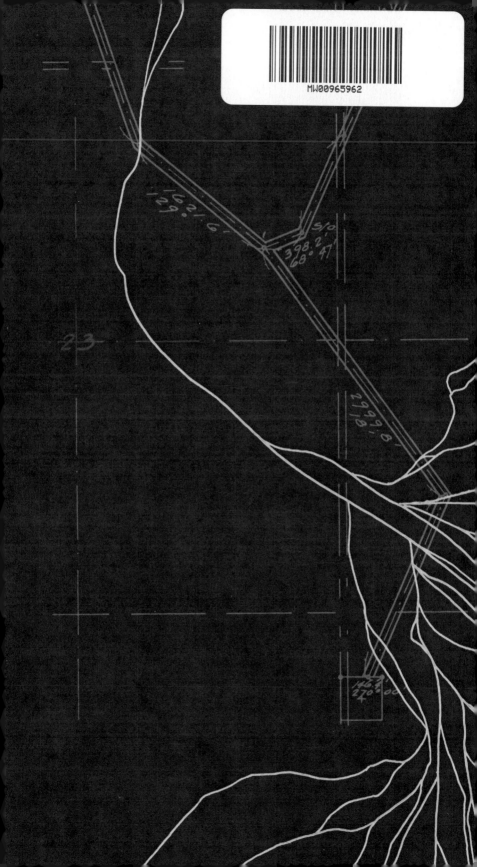

METASTASIS

NeWest Press

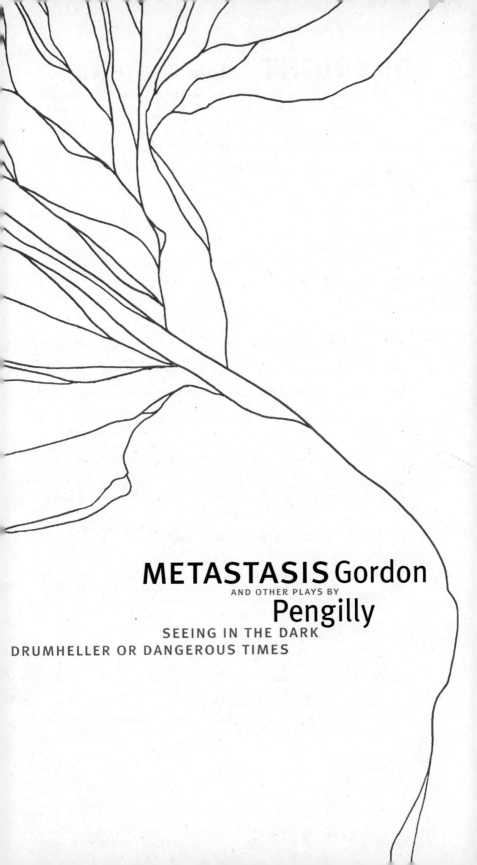

METASTASIS Gordon

AND OTHER PLAYS BY

Pengilly

SEEING IN THE DARK

DRUMHELLER OR DANGEROUS TIMES

Library and Archives Canada Cataloguing in Publication
Pengilly, Gordon, 1953-
        Metastasis and other plays / Gordon Pengilly.
(Prairie play series 27)
ISBN 978-1-897126-40-0
        I. Title. II. Series.
PS8581.E5532M48 2009   C812'.54   C2008-907090-9

Editor for the Board: Diane Bessai
Cover and interior design: Natalie Olsen
Author photo: Connie Zerger

Interior photos have been reproduced with the kind permission of their photographers.

Poetry permissions:
Excerpts from the poems "Lot" (p. 119 and 122), "One Night I Didn't Kill Myself" (p. 124), and "Bullets" (p. 124 – 125) are from *Flowers for Hitler* by Leonard Cohen © 1964. Published by McClelland & Stewart Ltd. Used with permission of the publisher. "I'm Nobody! Who Are You?" by Emily Dickinson (page 141) was reprinted from Public Domain.
All poems in *Seeing in the Dark* are written by the author and previously unpublished.

NeWest Press acknowledges the support of the Canada Council for the Arts, the Alberta Foundation for the Arts, and the Edmonton Arts Council for our publishing program. We also acknowledge the financial support of the Government of Canada through the Book Publishing Industry Development Program (BPIDP).

NeWest Press
201.8540.109 Street
Edmonton, Alberta T6G 1E6
780.432.9427
newestpress.com

No bison were harmed in the making of this book.
We are committed to protecting the environment and to the responsible use of natural resources. This book is printed on 100% recycled, ancient-forest-friendly paper.

1 2 3 4 5 12 11 10 09
Printed and bound in Canada

CONTENTS

PLAYWRIGHT'S INTRODUCTION

Writing is a form of dreaming. I'm thinking of those dreams, particularly the terrible ones, in which you can hear your own voice, there in the dark, reminding you that the dream isn't real. Don't be afraid, it isn't real, keep going. Go deeper, go darker, it'll be OK. You have some control of the action in those dreams, but not too much. Writing is like that. The goal is to tap the unconscious (or prick it or tickle it or whatever one does to channel the lyricism, the nuances, the more peculiar connections between things) while remaining conscious of the basic task, the construction of the story, more or less. The trick is to stay watchful and to let your mind wander at the same time. You don't want the left brain to know what the right brain is doing and vice versa. It's a balancing act. I don't know how I pull it off and I don't want to know.

I started writing when I was nine. I had a childhood illness and spent many months hospitalized over a three-year period. My aunt was an artist, pottery her specialty, but she also knew about drawing and watercolour. She showed me how to mix paints to make new tints and how to shade with charcoal to reveal contours and how to create a vanishing point. My mother gave me a book by John Nagy on how to draw horses and dogs, which I still have, and read me the plays she was always writing for church and community functions. My father brought me *National Geographic*. He was an avid reader of those beautiful books and I became one too. My first poems, which were descriptions of the photographs, were free and spare: "A white gorilla / is born / in captivity. It looks / like a clown and a ghost / put together." I played around with the length of lines and used a thesaurus to find words that were more unusual. I loved leaving those white spaces on the page to reveal stanzas. And some of my poems were more diary-like: "Four Calgary Stampeders / visited me / and wrote their names on my cast. I saw the Beatles / on Ed Sullivan / on the flat of my back." I heard my first radio play, *Old Yeller*, on a cold Sunday morning in December; it was dedicated to me by my brothers as a gift from home, and I remember how much it touched me.

I didn't know much about the theatre until I went to

university where I'd enrolled to play basketball, not to envisage my future, not really. I was still writing poetry, though, and by then some short stories too. I loved Thurber and Leacock. A student counsellor who looked like James Taylor encouraged me to take a drama class as an arts option: he said I needed some opening up. I fell for it: first acting and directing, then playwriting. Thurber had adapted his own short story, *The Secret Life of Walter Mitty*, into a play, so I did the same. My first play was based on a story I'd written about a boy who steals the neighbour's dog for someone to play with and then accidentally kills it. My drama professor said he liked it, so I left the basketball team in the middle of my sophomore year to spend more time writing and acting in plays. Life is full of quick pivots.

My poetry is nearly all serious and my short stories are nearly all humorous but, when I started writing plays, for some reason, I found myself mixing the two, the comic and sad or the comic and violent, the dire and hopeful, the funny and sur-real, trying to be ambiguous and intriguing. Well, it's easy to be ambiguous when you're young and don't know what you're doing. Harder to be intriguing. I went about trying to imitate Williams and Pinter and Shepard and Mamet and, gradually, somehow, came into my own voice. You start to realize that you can't imitate the greats without looking bad, it's inescapable, or without cheating yourself; and then you're halfway there. The other half takes your whole life.

I feel fortunate having started writing plays in the mid-70s, a great time for new theatre and playwriting across the country. I learned a tremendous amount about writing for the stage in the Drama Department at the University of Alberta from Ben Tarver, Jim DeFelice, and Sharon Pollock. I was the first MFA graduate in playwriting there, and it's also where several new theatre companies were born. Students Gerry Potter, Mark Manson, Stephen Heatley, Keith Digby, and Jan Selman all cre-ated their own companies or found work developing new plays with existing companies within a year or so after graduating. I was the first hired-on playwright with Theatre Network, on Workshop West's first Board of Directors, in Northern Light

Theatre's first playwrights unit. I was also Alberta Culture's
first script annotator and, while there, I created a new shelf
in their library for the few Canadian plays. The MFA program
offered me the opportunity to work with John Neville at the
Citadel, editing Brecht's *Schweyk in the Second World War*
for production, though mostly he just fed my soul with wild
stories about being in the theatre. I was further influenced by
the likes of John Murrell, Tom Hendry, David Fennario, Tom
Cone, Des McEnuff, and Bill Lane at the Banff Playwrights
Colony, which I attended several times in its early years. And
I wasn't the only young playwright on the ground floor of new
endeavours. Cutting their teeth around the same time were
Frank Moher, Gerald Reid, Raymond Storey, Connie Massing,
Michael McKinley, Brad Fraser, Vic Albert, and Paul Gross.
Impressive company.

My first professional show was a CBC radio production of my
one-act play *Seeds*, directed by Mark Schoenberg in 1977. The
play worked well on radio, and I remember saying to myself
how I'd like to do more of that. Eight years later I moved to
Calgary from Toronto (where I'd spent three years) to become
resident playwright with Theatre Calgary. I soon ran into
Martie Fishman, who was producing drama for CBC radio and,
over the next dozen years or so, we created some fifteen hours
of radio drama together. I love writing radio plays, sort of the
poor man's screenplay, the movie-in-your-ear, as it were, where
you can really go places and blow things up if you want to,
and for a fraction of the cost of making a movie. Being at the
bottom of the sea in a nuclear submarine is no more difficult to
produce than popping the top off a can of beer. And for those
of you who haven't ventured beyond *The Shadow* or *Jake and
the Kid* — well, you can't know how poetic and sophisticated and
experimental radio drama can be in the hands of people like
Pinter, Beckett, Stoppard, and Dylan Thomas.

I have adapted several of my stage plays to radio, television,
and the screen. You have to make a living, of course, and a good
story can have a wide life as well as a long one if you care enough
to learn a new craft. I learned about writing for radio through
practice. I learned about writing for television and film partly

from teaching it. Weird, but true. Mount Royal College had
hired me to teach scriptwriting in the newly formed Professional
Writing Program, and they wanted sections on all the scriptwriting forms. I said I could do it and started reading screen-
plays and teleplays like a madman and blasting through How To's
and industry magazines for structure and jargon and lore.

The passage of the playwright is grueling, the expectations
intimidating. Like all artists he is supposed to know what's
going on and to lead cutting edge discourse about it, and the
very good ones do. For example, Mamet says:

> When you come into the theater, you have to
> be willing to say that we're all here to undergo a
> communion, to find out what the hell is going on
> in this world. If you're not willing to say that, what
> you get is entertainment instead of art, and poor
> entertainment at that.

As a young playwright, statements like this unnerved me. I
had never felt that kind of pressure as a poet. My poems about
growing up on a farm, about my family and neighbours and
animals, about my love life and writer's life, about my aspira-
tions and nightmares, well, it never even occurred to me that
I might be expected to have any encompassing thought around
it all. If I did I wasn't conscious of it. Folks who work in the
theatre, out of necessity, I suppose, all clamour to find the
meaning in plays. The theatre is a very heady and cognizant
place and, for a long time, the fear of being inarticulate about
my ideas made me apprehensive and self-doubting. But slowly,
somehow, I turned that fear into nerve and my writing became
smarter and more liberated.

The meaning of a play, as Mamet implies, happens com-
munally, in and around the event "to order the universe into
a comprehensible form." However, the act of dramatizing,
of invention itself, is to look at the world in solitude. It can
be through an incident or calamity or some other kind of
dynamic, such as a relationship, a mystery, or a simple pos-
sibility. The task is to rearrange that thing: stretch it out or

compress it, dismantle it then put it back together again in new, often spontaneous ways. It matters privately first, little by little, until finally it gains its own life. After that it's up for grabs. In performance, a play becomes community property, interpreted, analyzed, and criticized for production and consumption. Not a walk in the park, to say the least.

I don't particularly like being asked what my plays are about. I can tell you the story if it has one, or sometimes I can tell you how I went about writing it. For instance, my house was broken into a while back. The place was ransacked, a back window broken, the dog under the bed, the smell of whisky and cigarettes in the air. It affected me more than I thought it would. I had trouble sleeping, I kept hearing things in the dark, I put a baseball bat by the door. After driving away from the house I would sometimes circle back to have a look down the alley. I knew that lightning wasn't likely to strike twice in the same place but it didn't seem to matter. And then, a few weeks after that, as if to confirm my mistrust of the world, I pulled up to a red light where a man got out of his car and came to my window and knocked. When I rolled it down he punched me. I suppose I must have cut him off or something, I don't know. I got out to confront the prick, but he'd gone and nobody came forward as a witness. So I began a new play. It became an inquiry into pervasive fear, wouldn't you know it, brought on by a random act of violence in a shadowy, crazy world where human separateness and despair and meaningless bonding are featured in various ways. I called it *Metastasis*.

Most of my plays have elements of paranoia, violence, or tragedy in them. My characters, who really aren't that bad, do bad things to each other which they deeply regret. They try to be forgiven, they work to redeem themselves, and in the process face up to themselves with varying degrees of success. My heroes give in to temptation all the time and suffer the consequences, occasionally rise above it, or sometimes receive unexpected rewards for their durability. The doctor in *Metastasis*, having lost out to his demons, ends up on a ledge gazing down at a parking lot only to be rescued by the person in the play he hurt most. He's been humiliated but is given another chance whether he deserves it or not. In *Drumheller or Dangerous Times* the troubled coalminer sees salvation in the dinosaur bone he discovers in his coalmine and sends for a paleontologist to affirm its value. The paleontologist falls in love with his girlfriend, which triggers some old bad blood and, when two strangers appear with a bag full of money, all hell breaks loose. Like the badlands they inhabit, these characters have become creatures well suited to survival, but deadly if stirred, and everyone gets hurt. *Seeing in the Dark* is the harshest of the plays in this book, if only because the main character is perhaps the most likeable. He is given to the worst behaviour while getting the cruellest treatment, some deserved and some not, and in the end he's alone and must be his own salvation.

The people in my plays want their lives to change but seem powerless to bring it about by acceptable means. Instead they find themselves making desperate stabs at it that inevitably fail. They're either clawing at the walls or walking around in half-awake, half-dreaming states. They have hallucinations and visions that they can articulate well enough, often quite beautifully, yet have trouble explaining themselves to each other about normal, essential things. I have tried to bring a kind of otherworldliness to the stage while remaining vital and real. It's hard to achieve that balance, but I keep working at it because it's central to my way of thinking about stories and how I create structure for them.

At the end of *Seeing in the Dark*, Clayton says: "My thoughts go round and round and so do the voices in my head…and my hopes and my dreams move in and out of the mist like grey wolves with mysterious eyes." That's pretty much how I think about writing. And the wolves take many shapes.

This collection is dedicated to my mother, Eva Pengilly, who has always believed in me.

Gordon Pengilly
Calgary
September 2008

SEEING IN THE DARK

A ONE-HOUR RADIO DRAMA

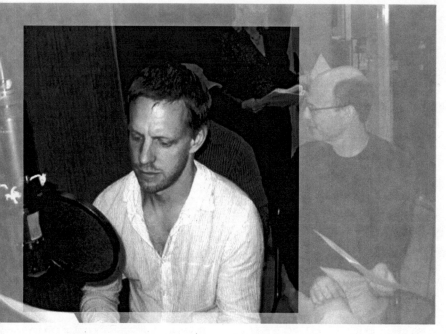

Trevor White (Clayton Sydora), Kerry Shale (Trevor Cameron), and Anne Edyvean (Producer/Director) during the 2007 BBC World Service production of *Seeing in the Dark*. (Lesley Allen)

SEEING IN THE DARK is the recipient of the 2007 BBC International Radio Drama Prize. It was produced in London, England for BBC World Service and aired worldwide in November 2007.

CAST

Clayton Sydora: Trevor White
Jerry Sydora/Greyhound bus driver/Prison official: Garrick Hagon
Candy Sydora: Buffy Davis
Donovan Sydora: Nathan Nolan
Trevor Cameron/Bad man from Manitoba: Kerry Shale
Ruby: Barbara Barnes
Wade/Bobby Baron/Bad man from Manitoba: Simon Lee Philips
Jodie: Lisa Came
Tracy: Joannah Tincey
Inmate (Henry)/Old guard: Peter Marinker

PRODUCTION

Producer/Director: Anne Edyvean
Original Music: Nicolai Abrahamsen
Technical Production: Graham Harper
Production Coordinator: Lesley Allen

MAIN CHARACTERS

Clayton Sydora, 21 (and 26)
Their parents Jerry and Candy, mid-40s
His brother, Donovan, 17
Trevor Cameron, Clayton's counsellor, 50s
Ruby, a stranger on the bus, 30

SUPPORTING CHARACTERS

Wade, a cab driver, 20s
Jodie, Clayton's girlfriend, 21
Tracy, Donovan's girlfriend, 15
Father (50s) and his son (30s) on the bus
Greyhound bus driver
Two bad men from Manitoba, 20s
Bobby Baron, Jodie's new lover, 20s
Prison official
Old guard
Inmate (Henry)

ONE

Clayton: *V.O.* I'm telling you this as if I understand it all.

Music: under.

Clayton: *V.O.* But I know that I don't. I've put this together out of memories and nightmares and there'll certainly been time enough to see what it all really means, now that I'm alone again in the dark.

Sound: the sea rises up, seagulls, a distant ship's horn.

Clayton: *V.O.* The sea that you hear is not my sea. It's Donovan's sea but it's in my imagination. Donovan's my brother who is four years younger than me, who I haven't seen for two years. He sent me a postcard today from Tofino on Vancouver Island with a picture of a beach and a rainforest and a slice of blue ocean and on the back of it he wrote that he has met a girl and they are both working at a little café and saving up their money to go to Cancun and he says that he is happy.

Sound: interior, prison, an inmate singing. It echoes against the prison brick as if from the bottom of a well.

Clayton: *V.O.* I'm twenty-six years old now and I've never been to the sea. I found a book in the prison library, though, that has some poems in it about the sea, and about a lot of other things, too, that are as deep and powerful as the sea, like love and death and redemption and suffering, and I have memorized some of them, for it passes the time:

> The night of the doomed, the pale moon appears
> With heart-wrenching gloom, with its basins of woe,
> See the star-dazzled sleep of the shipwrecked souls
> In the eye of the storm on the dog-tired sea.
> Now at dawn — the voices of those on the wind,
> All the howling and booming, aloft in the salt sheet,
> They break on the crag and we hear them distinctly:
> That one my father and that one my blue-eyed brother.

Sound: the singing and the sea fade away.

Clayton: *V.O.* I hear voices too.

Sound: an inmate crying nearby.

Clayton: *V.O.* He always cries at this time of night. It's a gentle sort of crying and it's becoming gentler with the passing of the months. He's a Blackfoot from the reserve outside of Fort McLeod. He doesn't talk very much but then neither do I. I'm in the quiet time of my life it would seem, quiet on the outside, and on the inside I let the sounds come and go and the voices come and go however they want to. The soft voice of my brother mingles with the words of the poet and the sound of the sea chimes with the laughter of my girlfriend like a clear, clear bell and the voices of my mother and father fight like two dogs in the dead of night and the voice of my counsellor tells me that everything is going to be all right.

Music: transition.

Clayton: *V.O.* Five years ago now…

Sound: interior, visitors' room, others in random conversation (background).

Trevor: How are you, Clayton?

Clayton: Oh, I'm slowly going crazy, Trevor. But I guess I shouldn't say that. You might get me put in the padded room.

Trevor: Well, I know you by now. I know how your mind works.

Clayton: You *think* you do.

Trevor: I've got some good news for you.

Clayton: Oh yeah?

Trevor: You're being paroled. They're taking three months off your sentence. You're free to go in two weeks. *Beat.* You don't look happy.

Clayton: Why are they doing this?

Trevor: You have to learn to trust the system once in awhile, son. I've been going to bat for you, I've been writing some letters and making some calls.

Clayton: Since when?

Trevor: Since the day we met, or nearly. Since the day I started to believe in you.

Clayton: In two weeks, eh?

Trevor: We have to get you ready. You have to make a list of things to do when you get out, a set of guidelines for starting your life over again. You can make it as long as you want to but it has to be realistic and I have to be able to sign off on it.

Clayton: Who's going to see this list?

Trevor: Just me and you.

Clayton: Then I guess it better to be a good one, huh?

Trevor: You have a lot of potential, Clayton. This is the last time we're going to see you in here. You're going to carve out a life for yourself that can be admired. Let's shake on it.

Clayton: Okay, Trevor. You've been good to me. Here's my hand.

Music: under.

Clayton: *V.O.* I never thought of myself as having potential. It just wasn't a word I would've used for myself. I would've used cocky, though. And if cocky is just another word for a kind of confidence and if confidence means that I'm not too afraid of the future, then perhaps potential wasn't far off the mark. So I worked on my list of things to do. I took it seriously and I tried to be realistic and when my counsellor came back in a few days we talked about it and we narrowed it down to five things.

Sound: visitors' room as before.

Clayton: *To Trevor, who adlibs encouragement.* Okay, so my list goes like this: to find a good job. To start some kind of hobby that doesn't involve booze or drugs or guns. To make sure my brother is doing okay and if he isn't to do something about it. To make my apologies to the people I've hurt or disappointed, and last, to forgive those who have hurt or disappointed me.

Sound: a buzzer to end their visit.

Trevor: See you tomorrow, Clayton.

Clayton: *V.O.* It all sounded so simple.

Sound: inmate singing again, sadly, echoing against the prison brick.

Old guard: *Distant.* Quiet in the block!

Sound: the clang of cells being auto-locked.

Clayton: Under the midday sun in the desiccated wind, far-flung.

Old guard: *Closer.* Lights out!

Clayton:

> On the wing of the wandering gull, on the unsung sea,
> Their voices are voyagers, ghostly, beseeching me:
> Lift your sails and follow! Point your boat to wide red rim!
> And who am I to argue? My journey to begin I must obey,
> For all I am is a dream midst the unending waves.

Old guard: *Close by; kindly.* Lights out, Clayton. That's a good boy.

TWO

Clayton: *V.O.* On the day of my release it rained hard.

Sound: thunder.

Clayton: *V.O.* Torrents came down and the wind was heavy and the sky was wild and grey. I have always loved storms, the kind a man can lean against, a bracing wind and a wet, stiff wind, and thunder and lightning and fearsomeness.

Prison official: Have you got everything?

Clayton: Yes, sir. I've got everything.

Prison official: Are your mom and dad picking you up?

Clayton: No, sir, Mr. Cameron is. That's his car right out there, I think.

Prison official: Well, good luck to you, Clayton.

Clayton: Oh, I'll need more than luck, sir, but I won't turn luck away that's for sure.

Prison official: *Turns his head.* One for release!

Sound: an automated metal gate slides open — more thunder — and then the gate slides shut again and closes with a solid bang.

Clayton: *V.O.* Once or twice in my life I'd felt torn in half by opposite forces that were somehow immobilizing and for a moment as I stood there outside the prison gate with the whole world in front of me that feeling came again and it was almost unbearable. I could not turn back and I could not step forward. The wind and the rain lashed at my cheek and my heart was banging in my throat and by hell I was going to cry and I couldn't stop it from coming.

Sound: a car horn beeps.

Trevor: *Distant.* Clayton! Over here!

Clayton: *V.O.* But I swallowed it back as best as I could and I walked away from the prison.

Music: transition.
Sound: interior, a car, the slash and knock of windshield wipers.

Trevor: You know I'd give you a ride home, Clayton. All you have to do is ask.

Clayton: Greyhound's fine. Thanks anyway.

Trevor: Did you talk to your mom and dad?

Clayton: No, just to my brother. He offered to come up and get me but I told him the bus ride would do me some good. You know — get my head on straight, think about my list of things to do.

Trevor: It's going to take you a while to fit back in.

Clayton: I'll be okay.

Trevor: You have my number, right? I want you to call me whenever you feel like it. Any time of day, for any reason at all, okay?

Clayton: Don't be a mother hen.

Trevor: I want you to call me in a week. Will you do that?

Clayton: Jeez, Trevor.

Trevor: If you don't call me I'll be worried.

Clayton: I'll do it. I'll call you.

Trevor: Good.

Sound: car slows and its signal light clicks.

Trevor: How long does it take to get to your hometown from here by bus?

Clayton: Oh, the milk run takes about six hours, I guess.

Trevor: Do you have enough money for something to eat?

Clayton: I'm okay.

Trevor: I could lend you some.

Clayton: You're going to drive me crazy, Trevor. Just drop me off right here, that's fine.

Sound: car pulls over and stops.

Trevor: You take care of yourself, son. Here's your ticket.

Clayton: Thanks.

Trevor: If that job with your friend doesn't go right you let me know and I'll help you find something else.

Clayton: *As he climbs out.* What could go wrong?

Trevor: Keep your nose clean!

Clayton: Yeah, yeah.

Sound: car door closes.

Clayton: *V.O.* And that was that. It was four o'clock in the afternoon on a Thursday in May and the rain had stopped.

Sound: car honks and drives away.

Clayton: *V.O.* It was the first day of the rest of my life, which seemed a bit pathetic right then because between me and the door of the bus stood a puddle of water with the sun shining in it and when I stepped in it —

Sound: boot steps into puddle of water.

Clayton: *V.O.* — the sun stuck to the toe of my boot and went up the stairs with me like something a clown would notice.

THREE

Sound: interior, the drone of a Greyhound bus and the indistinct conversation between two men of which we only catch the occasional word.

Clayton: *V.O.* For nearly an hour I'd been eavesdropping. Two men, a father and his son, talking about a family crisis that had happened. Couldn't quite get the hang of it though, couldn't figure out who the victim was, kept drifting in and out of it in the hum of the tires on the highway.

Sound: the bus abruptly drops down a gear and the engine starts to pull.

Clayton: *V.O.* We came to a little town on a hill. The bus depot was inside of a Western and Chinese food café. There was a sign in the window: "Have you seen this dog?" with a picture of the dog, and the dog looked a lot like me.

Sound: the bus slows to a stop; the door opens with a gasp.

Bus driver: *Intercom.* Big Valley. Ten minutes.

Sound: exterior, the bus idles.

Clayton: *V.O.* I got out to stretch my legs. The air felt good in the after-rain. I'd quit smoking in jail but I suddenly wanted one again. The father and son were smoking behind the bus. I moved closer to them with my hands in my pockets and my nose in the air.

Father: *Fading up.* She never did come over. She was afraid I might ask her a few questions.

Son: She would've lied about it.

Father: Yes, of course, but the eyes don't lie. She never *could* lie to me, you know. Well, we could never really lie to each other and that's the truth.

Son: And now she's gone.

Father: Unrepentant.

Son: But not understood.

Father: *To Clayton.* Did you want something, boy?

Clayton: No, sir, I don't want anything.

Son: He sure looks like he wants something.

Father: You came on the bus at Drumheller.

Clayton: That's right.

Father: We came on at Bassano. We're coming from a funeral. What're *you* coming from?

Sound: the bus revs up a bit.

Clayton: *V.O.* I'm coming from hell, I want to say and almost do. But I don't say anything. I have intruded upon their little mystery, their dismal affair, and they know who I am, not by name or by number, but by the tightness in my shoulders and the wolf in my eyes.

Sound: the bus horn honks to summon its passengers.

Clayton: *V.O.* So when I climbed back onto the bus I found another seat, one at the tail-end, and I put my jacket in the window to block out the setting sun and I said to myself that I'd catch a little nap. I'm like a child who closes his eyes so he won't be seen.

Sound: the whoosh of heavy brakes releasing and the bus moves forward.

FOUR

Music: transition.
Sound: interior, the bus drones.

Clayton: *V.O.* We had stopped at another little town and a woman had gotten on and she had come to the back of the bus, passing up several empty seats until she stood in the aisle above me—

Ruby: Can I sit here?

Clayton: *V.O.* — and I shifted my weight and I put my duffle bag under my feet.

Ruby: Thanks.

Clayton: *V.O.* She was older than me, maybe thirty. She smelled faintly of tobacco and perfume and perspiration, a nice combination, not a bad one, and though I wanted to be alone I couldn't help gazing at her legs.

Ruby: It's humid in here.

Clayton: *V.O.* Well it wasn't on my list of the things to do to get laid as quickly as possible, and besides, she had a wedding ring on her finger, so we rode side by side for an hour without speaking.

Sound: the bus gears down as it goes up a hill.

Clayton: *V.O.* She opened her purse and took out some gum. Her nails were painted.

Ruby: Want some?

Clayton: No thanks. Yeah, okay. What the hell. Thanks.

Sound: wrapping paper.

Ruby: Where are you coming from?

Clayton: Drumheller.

Ruby: I had a friend who lived there. I don't know what happened to her, one day she just disappeared. Ran off, I guess. Is that where you live?

Clayton: No. *Beat.*

Ruby: So where are you going to?

Clayton: Home. Little town in the foothills, you've probably never heard of it.

Ruby: *Muses.* A little town in the foothills.

Clayton: *V.O.* She smiled to herself, vaguely mocking me, I thought, and I decided I wouldn't talk to her anymore and I put my head against the window and pretended to sleep and I could hear her chewing her gum in a teasing sort of way it seemed to me and I shifted my weight away from her.

Ruby: Would you like me to go and sit somewhere else so you can stretch out?

Clayton: No, that's okay.

Ruby: I can never sleep on buses. I try but I fail. *Beat.* I like your tattoo. *Beat.*

Clayton: I got it in prison — I'm just getting out.

Ruby: Oh, I knew that.

Clayton: How? Is there a sign on my forehead?

Ruby: *Little laugh.* Well, nearly. No, I'm a mind-reader. I'm reading your mind right now.

Clayton: What am I thinking?

Ruby: You're thinking about your girlfriend.

Clayton: You should go into show business. Or get a job with the police. They hire people like you, you know, to track down missing children.

Ruby: No, I can only do tricks like that when I'm in a good mood. Missing children make me sad.

Clayton: Well I'm glad you're in a good mood.

Ruby: Is that how I seem?

Clayton: No.

She laughs again. Beat.

Ruby: How long were you in for?

Clayton: Eighteen months.

Ruby: What did you do?

Clayton: I held up a liquor store. Actually I held up three of them, all in one night. I was really stoned, I felt invincible. It wasn't my first offense but it was the first time I'd ever used a gun.

Ruby: Oh, I see.

Clayton: My counsellor said it's good for me to talk about it.

Ruby: What's it like?

Clayton: Prison?

Ruby: No, to hold something up with a gun. Do you get a big kick out of it?

Clayton: Yeah, you do. It's crazy, I mean it's all mixed up, you know, with excitement and anger and shame...

Ruby: You must've had a good counsellor.

Clayton: Yeah — he'd been down the road. He could reach in.

Ruby: *Muses.* Reach in.

Clayton: He helped me make a list of things to do, a set of guidelines for starting my whole life over again. The first one is getting a job. I have an old friend in my hometown who owns his own body shop now so I called him up and he said he could use me. I love working on cars. The second thing on my list is to get a hobby that doesn't involve booze or drugs or guns.

Ruby: Well, that narrows it down, eh?

Clayton: I have an idea for it.

Ruby: What is it?

Clayton: When we were kids my brother and I taught ourselves taxidermy. I stole a book from the town library that described how to do it and we used to go out and pick up road kill from the highway to practice on, you know, rabbits and squirrels, all sorts of birds, an owl, a pheasant, some crows. I was just getting good at it then one night my dad got mad and he burned up the book and all of our equipment.

Ruby: Why did he get mad?

Clayton: He drinks too much. Anyway, I was thinking I might take it up again. *Beat.*

Ruby: Do you know what you call a flock of starlings?

Clayton: No, what?

Ruby: An exultation. You call them an exultation of starlings. That's really pretty, isn't it?

Clayton: Yeah. It is. *Beat.* Do you know what you call a flock of crows?

Ruby: No.

Clayton: You call them a murder of crows.

Sound: the bus gears down as it goes up another hill.

Clayton: What's your name?

Ruby: It's Ruby.

Clayton: Where are you going to, Ruby? Ruby Tuesday. Ruby who chews spearmint gum, Ruby who looks sort of sad...

Ruby: You think you can charm me with crap like that?

Clayton: Can I?

Ruby: Can you wake the dead?

Clayton: What does it take and I'll try.

Ruby: You tell me then we'll both know.

Clayton: *V.O.* We talked for more than an hour and it had grown nearly dark outside. She. Beside me, smelling faintly of tobacco and perfume and perspiration. And when I put my arm around her, her hair, another nice smell. And when. And when I lowered the zipper of her jacket a warm waft of air and a mixture of new smells and her breasts looked so soft...

Ruby: *Whispers.* When I was a girl I had flying dreams.

Clayton: *V.O.* ...which I touch. And I put my lips to her ear and I put my hand on her thigh...

Ruby: But I don't anymore.

Clayton: *V.O.* And I put my hand between her legs...

Ruby: Why *is* that?

Clayton: *V.O.* I say I don't know, I don't know why people stop having flying dreams, and I'm undoing her blue jeans now but she stops me and she says in my ear...

Ruby: Wait a minute then come in.

Clayton: *V.O.* And she leaves her seat and she goes into the washroom and I wait for a minute and I go into the washroom to be with her and I lock the door behind me. I finish undoing her jeans and she lifts up her top and we kiss and she puts her hand inside my zipper. And I lift up her arms and leave them there and I turn her around like a ballerina in a closet and I lower her blue jeans. *Beat.*

> This girl of the tulips, oh pressure of pigeons;
> I feel intoxicated!
> My soul is a bird full of brandy
> And her mouth is the essence of a plum.
> And today I do not fear death:
> I've gained passage into living and breathing!

Music: transition.
Sound: the Blackfoot inmate gently cries again, and further away, the other inmate sings, his voice reverberating on the prison brick.

Clayton: *V.O.* No, it wasn't on my list of things to do to get laid as soon as I could but sometimes things just happen and afterwards she cried, and when I tried to comfort her she pushed me away and we did not speak again until we arrived at the next little town on the milk run home.

Sound: interior, bus idling.

Bus driver: *Intercom.* Elnora. Twenty minutes.

Clayton: You don't even know my name.

Ruby: I don't need to know your name. You don't know mine either. Ruby just came to me.

Clayton: Why did you cry?

Ruby: Because.

Clayton: Because why? Is it because you're married that you cried?

Ruby: I've told so many lies I don't remember what the truth is anymore.

Clayton: Everybody tells lies — you have to sometimes — the whole truth could kill a person.

Ruby: But it's bigger than that.

Clayton: What do you mean?

Clayton: *V.O.* And right then I look up and I see the bus driver making his way back toward us. He has his eyes glued to me and Ruby sees him too and she puts her hand on my leg. Her hand is as light as a sparrow.

Bus driver: You two. I've had a complaint.

Clayton: *V.O.* And it's quivering like one too.

Bus driver: We have codes of conduct in here and you know what I'm talking about. You're a woman so you can stay but you — you collect your things and you get off.

Clayton: Your codes of conduct can kiss my ass.

Bus driver: Two minutes — say goodbye. If you're not off by then I'm calling the cops. *As he leaves.* And I know you don't want *that*.

Clayton: He knows where I've been — you'd think he could cut me some slack.

Ruby: I'll get off with you. It's an adventure.

Clayton: No, that's okay. You have somewhere to get to.

Ruby: No, I have somewhere to get away from but I don't have somewhere to get to, not really. We can get a room in a hotel like sweethearts. We'll order up some pizza and watch TV and make love in a real bed.

Clayton: *V.O.* And she took my hand in both of hers and her eyes were filled with tears again and all of her various smells were in the air and one of them was desperation.

Ruby: I want to be with you!

Clayton: *V.O.* And she clung to me and I had to pry myself away.

FIVE

Music: under.

Clayton: *V.O.* The bus depot here was in a hotel so I threw my duffle bag over my shoulder like a sailor and as I walked toward the door I was conscious that Ruby might be watching me and when I got to the door I looked back but I could not see her. No movie goodbyes. No last wave as the ship pulls out.

Sound: the bus drives away.

Clayton: *V.O.* Just as well, I thought. But my heart was aching.

Sound: interior, a key opens a door and then the door closes.

Clayton: *V.O.* I went to a liquor store and I bought a bottle of whiskey and a six-pack of beer and I bought a sandwich in the restaurant and I went up to my room and I lay down on the bed to watch some TV.

Sound: a television sitcom; canned, mocking laughter.

Clayton: *V.O.* I had a few drinks and I ate up my sandwich and I decided to call home. It was nine o'clock at night.

Sound: telephone ringing.

Donovan: *Answers phone.* Hello?

Clayton: Hi, Donovan. It's me.

Donovan: Hey! Are you back in town?

Clayton: No, I won't get there until tomorrow sometime. Long story. Are mom and dad there?

Donovan: No, I'm alone. Dad went to the bar and mom went down to the 7-11 for some cigarettes. They had a big fight tonight.

Clayton: What about?

Donovan: I don't know, everything, you know.

Clayton: Are you okay?

Donovan: Yeah.

Clayton: *V.O.* Said the one with the red mustache.

Man 2: Family thing.

Man 1: A wedding. A sister. She married a farmer. *Beat.*

Clayton: *V.O.* Prison teaches you things. You get quick for sizing people up. Know the situation, know the relative danger, the possibilities. Who has a grudge, who has a knife. Who is losing his mind. These two in the car. Something not right, not clear. The taste of metal in my mouth. Am waiting for the next thing to happen and here it is.

Man 2: I have to take a leak. Turn off here. Up over that hill.

Sound: the car slows and turns onto gravel.

Man 2: You don't mind, eh?

Clayton: No.

Sound: the car goes a little further and then slows to a stop; the engine idles.

Man 2: That's good. Nobody can see my pecker from the highway from here.

Sound: the car door opens up.

Clayton: *V.O.* He opens the door but he doesn't get out. Instead he turns around to me — and there's a gun in his hand which he points at me — but I'm ready for him and I'm already reaching for his wrist which I grab with both of my hands and push it forward and the gun goes off and blows a clean hole in the side of the driver's head.

nd: gunshot; reverberating, ringing.

breeze *O.* His voice echoing, doubling over itself. I rip the gun

Clayton. and the gunshot is ringing in my ears I grab the

tho llar pull it back against his throat put the gun

both

thun

wind

Mus.

bite to

Clayton.

Sound: a car c

Man 2: *Te*   *to?*

Clayton: Get out!

Clayton: *V.O.* He gets out and I get out through the door right behind him I still have a grip on his collar he's shaking like a leaf and he pisses himself.

Man 2: Don't shoot me! I'm sorry!

Clayton: Lay down in the ditch on your belly!

Man 2: Oh no! Oh no!

Clayton: *V.O.* He lies down in the ditch I go back to the car I pull the guy with the hole in his head over to the passenger's side and I shut the door...

Sound: door slams.

Clayton: *V.O.* ...and then I run around to the driver's side and I crawl in under the wheel...

Sound: the other door opens and closes.

Clayton: *V.O.* ...and I drive off.

Sound: tires spit gravel and the car speeds off.

SIX

Music: plaintively under.

Clayton: *V.O.*

> I'm used to eating strange things
> From the deep blue sea;
> I have a preference for turtles.
> All my life I've gone shirtless —
> My body all bronzed
> And my hair bleached blonde.
> I have been torn into pieces
> By the wind and the seasons
> And have sewn myself up again
> With old nails and string.
> Now we must talk of other things:
> Of oblivion and demons.

Sound: interior, car on gravel road.

Clayton: *V.O.* I knew this backcountry west of the highway quite well, where rough secondary roads lead into the Clearwater Hills and vanish like veins into the crags and the shadows of the Barrier Range. I used to come up this way to hunt deer with my dad and my uncle when I was fourteen, fifteen, before I got my first car and before my dad started drinking so much and beating me. It was a beautiful day.

Sound: the car slows down and stops.

Clayton: *V.O.* The man with no hair and long neck had bled well. There was blood on the seat and on the floor and his brains were on the window beside me.

Sound: door opens and he gets out — birds are chirping and insects buzzing — indeed it's a beautiful day.

Clayton: *V.O.* I had only seen one dead man before this day, not counting those in caskets. The man who shared my cell in the first days of my incarceration chewed into his own wrist for the vein that would end it all and I had woken from a dream about my beautiful girlfriend to find his bloody arm dangling in my face from the bunk above me.

Sound: the passenger door opens and he drags the dead man out.

Clayton: *V.O.* I had driven westward for over an hour until the road gave out near a creek and it was here that I dumped the body. The car had seat covers on and I took them off and I pulled out the floor mats and I wiped the whole car down using creek water and the shirt off the man. The gun was a really nice browning 9 MM, probably worth four or five hundred dollars and I wiped it down for fingerprints and I reared back and threw it as far as I could but when I looked down at the end of my arm the gun was still in my hand. I have always loved guns. So I put it in my duffle bag and drove away.

Music: transition.

Clayton: *V.O.* I went eastward, changing roads as I came upon them and finally got back to the highway which I crossed and then drove to the nearest town. I was sure the car was stolen and I wanted no part of it so I parked it in the empty lot behind the community hockey arena and left the keys inside, then I walked downtown to the local watering hole and phoned home again.

Sound: phone rings.

Candy: *Answers.* Hello?

Operator: *Recorded.* Please deposit two dollars and sixty-five cents for the first two minutes.

Sound: coins dropping into pay phone.

Clayton: Hi, mom. It's Clayton.

Candy: *Excited.* Where are you? Donovan said you'd phoned. We didn't know you were getting out when you did or we would've come up to get you.

Clayton: They surprised me, I barely had time to call.

Candy: You got out for good behaviour, huh?

Clayton: I guess so, mom. Something like that.

Candy: So where *are* you?

Clayton: I got a ride with a friend down to Calgary.

Candy: I'll jump in the car right now.

Clayton: No, listen, just send Donovan. It'll give us some time to talk, you know, brother stuff. Is he there? Put him on.

Candy: Okay, well maybe you're right. *Calls.* Donovan! *Back to Clayton.* I've got one of my migraines today and it's killing me. *Calls again.* Donovan! It's your brother! *Back to Clayton.* We're glad you're coming home, Clayton. We'll have a big party or something.

Clayton: No, mom, I don't want a party.

Candy: Here's your brother. *To Donovan.* He only has a minute or so.

Sound: telephone changes hands.

Donovan: Hi.

Clayton: Can you come and get me?

Donovan: Sure. Where at?

Clayton: I told mom I was in Calgary but I'm actually over in Irricana. Long story. Is dad there too?

Donovan: No, he had to work late, he won't be home until after supper.

Clayton: Did you tell him I called yesterday?

Donovan: Yeah, mom did.

Clayton: What did he say?

Donovan: Nothing much.

Clayton: I'll be in the tavern.

Donovan: Okay.

SEVEN

Music: under.

Clayton: *V.O.* I have been drawn to extreme opposites since I can remember. I work hard and play hard. I love hard and hate hard. I don't know why I started breaking the law because I've always liked having a job. My counsellor said that I might be bi-polar and it's true that I can't stay focused for very long and it's my tendency to go to the edges for relief. There's medication I could be taking that might help me to stay in the middle but I'm afraid to try it. Instead I have medicated myself with booze and drugs and cars and sex and when I'm not pacing the room like a caged animal I have wonderful daydreams about long grasses and mountain streams and wild horses and wolves.

Sound: tavern, a game of pool (background).

Donovan: *Approaching.* Hi there.

Clayton: You made it.

Sound: a chair pulls out and he sits.

Donovan: How are you?

Clayton: I'm okay. You've put on some pounds. Are you taller? Are you trying to grow a beard?

Donovan: I'm lifting weights — I don't think I'm any taller.

Clayton: Is your pecker any bigger?

Donovan: Way bigger. *Clayton laughs.* The bouncer asked me for ID. So I told him I was just coming in to get you, I'm not supposed to be sitting.

Clayton: Let's just go then. I've got some beer in my bag for the road. Give me a smoke.

Donovan: I thought you quit.

Clayton: I started again.

Donovan: When?

Clayton: Just now. Give me a hug. Your brother's back.

Sound: interior, car on highway, music on, radio under.

Clayton: *V.O.* I tell him about the men who tried to rob me but not about the man who was shot in the head. I badly want to but I know it's better that he never knows. I show him the gun, though, and he whistles at it, then we turn to other things that are normal and not too violent and not too unhappy.

Clayton: I hear you have a girlfriend.

Donovan: Who told you that?

Clayton: It was in one of mom's letters. Is she pretty? Do you love her?

Donovan: Maybe I do. I like her a lot. But there's a problem. Well, actually there's two problems. The first problem is her father is really crazy and the second problem is she's only fifteen.

Clayton: That's a good way to get shot.

Donovan: Yeah, I know it is, so that's why we're going to run away together.

Clayton: Don't.

Donovan: Why not?

Clayton: They'll track you down that's why.

Donovan: No, they won't. We just need some more money and then we can hide better. I've got that part-time job at Blockbuster and she's getting some money from her aunt when she dies.

Clayton: When's she going to die?

Donovan: She's got cancer really bad, it won't be long.

Clayton: Well maybe by then you'll decide it's better not to run away because once you start running it's really hard to stop. Believe me I know. *Beat.* And speaking of women, how's Jodie doing? Do you ever see her?

Donovan: Sometimes, not much. She's working out at the Husky in the diner.

Clayton: *Beat.* There's something you're not telling me. What? Come on.

Donovan: Well I heard she's dating someone.

Clayton: Who?

Donovan: I honestly don't know, I just heard it.

Music: radio tune stretches out into something more abstract.

Clayton: *V.O.* Jodie was my girlfriend. It hadn't been going very well between us during those days before I went off to prison and it didn't get any better once I got inside. We wrote a couple of letters and she came up to see me at Christmastime and we talked on the phone a few times but we always just ended up fighting or crying and finally she said that she didn't want to talk to me again until she'd thought things over and when I asked her if she'd at least wait for me until I got out to make any big decisions she said that she probably would. Well that was six months ago and we still hadn't talked and I was still harbouring some hope for us. But if it was true she'd fallen for someone else I couldn't see myself sticking around even though I had a job to go to and even though I hadn't dealt with forgiveness yet.

Donovan: I've got your car running pretty good, eh?

Clayton: *V.O.* And then there was Donovan to see to.

Donovan: Dad didn't believe I could do it by myself but I showed the bugger, eh?

Clayton: How's it been between you and him?

Donovan: It's been okay. *Beat.*

Clayton: I know when you're lying, brother. Is he hurting you?

Donovan: No. Not really. *Beat.*

Clayton: *V.O.* I decided not to push him, I could tell it was making him nervous, I could feel it coming off him like heat. We rolled into town at about eight-thirty and my head started hurting and my stomach started feeling funny and I remembered my counsellor saying how hard it would be to fit back in and I suddenly couldn't go home. So I had Donovan drop me off at the motel downtown and I said I'd see them all tomorrow for breakfast. He had a hard time letting me go and I could see in his eyes the old ghosts forming up that made him so sad and so introverted and I kicked myself for being so selfish as he drove off.

EIGHT

Clayton: *V.O.*
> Out of dense back-country unknown to him
> The deserter stumbles. With bloodied fist knocks
> At the first door he comes upon, for a morsel
> To eat and a corner to sleep in. But the house
> Is strange territory and at night he sees ghosts
> And hears gunfire, and his blood-streaked face
> Cannot hide the poor youth who peers out.

Candy: Where's Clayton?

Clayton: *V.O.* This is what I imagine. I'm a fly on the wall of the kitchen in the house I grew up in.

Donovan: He's at the motel.

Candy: I don't understand.

Clayton: *V.O.* The kitchen table, the linoleum.

Donovan: He said he wanted to be alone tonight.

Candy: We're his family!

Clayton: *V.O.* The wooden chairs and the wooden cupboards and the old metal basin and the calendar from Maxwell's Garage on the fridge and the poor yellow light.

Jerry: We're not good enough for him, I guess.

Candy: Don't get started, Jerry.

Jerry: I'll start if I want to.

Candy: How is he, Donovan? What did he say?

Donovan: He's fine. He said he has a list of things to do and he says he has some plans going on.

Jerry: Are they going on in the light of day or are they going on in the deep, dark shadows.

Candy: Jerry, have a heart.

Jerry: Shut your trap.

Candy: You're drunk.

Donovan: I'm going to go eat in my room.

Jerry: You're going sit at table and listen to me.

Candy: Leave him alone.

Jerry: Shut up!

Donovan: I'm just going to eat in my room, I'm not trying to cause anything.

Jerry: Do you know what I did when Clayton got sent to jail — I actually cried for joy — because I was hoping you'd get old enough not to be influenced by him when he got out, but I guess they didn't keep him in there long enough, did they.

Donovan: I'm just going to eat in my room and watch TV.

Candy: I have such a terrible headache tonight.

Jerry: You can all go to hell!

Clayton: *V.O.*

> Oh Lord — for just a few hours of sleep
> Without fear. Let sleep take the voices away,
> The guilt and the shame all away, or return me
> To the back-country to gratefully perish.

NINE

Sound: interior, a car door closes and the car starts to move.

Cab driver: Where to, pal?

Clayton: *V.O.* I was going crazy in my motel room so I called for a cab and I recognize the driver right off and in a second or two he recognizes me.

Wade: Well, damn. Is that you, Clayton?

Clayton: Hello, Wade.

Wade: When did you get home?

Clayton: Oh, about an hour ago is all.

Wade: How are you?

Clayton: I'm okay.

Wade: You look different. What is it?

Clayton: I shaved my beard off, maybe that's it.

Wade: Yeah, maybe that is.

Clayton: *V.O.* We'd all been best of friends, he and Bobby Baron and I. We'd drunk a lot of liquor together and chased a lot of girls together and gotten into trouble together and he was looking at me in the rearview mirror and he was hunting my eyes for a clue.

Clayton: I've been in prison, Wade. It'll change a person some.

Wade: Are you going to stick around for a while?

Clayton: I have a job to go to so I reckon I will. I'm going to be working with Bobby over at his new body shop.

Wade: *Carefully.* Is that so?

Clayton: How are things with you?

Wade: Well I got married to a girl from Water Valley, Clay, and we have a little boy already, and I guess I don't think I've ever been happier. I'm driving cab for the Maxwell's part-time and I'm taking a course on the internet for starting up a small business and we're going to get a little antique shop going.

Clayton: That sounds really good, Wade.

Wade: Yeah, I guess I couldn't be any happier. So where can I take you?

Clayton: Out to the Husky station.

Wade: Right.

Sound: the car speeds up.

Clayton: *V.O.* It had been Wade who'd introduced me to Jodie.

Party music under.

Clayton: *V.O.* We'd gone to the local stockcar races and demolition derby and at the end of the day there was a barbeque and dance on the track which was customary and he ran into Jodie who he knew through another girl and we all four danced and had a few beers and Jodie and I ended up in bed together and that's all it took. I told her I'd had a few problems with the law but that I hadn't been in jail for more than a night or two at a time and she found something sweet in that, she said. She was a bit on the wild side herself and there were a few stories about her. I learned she could drink with anyone on the planet, which duly impressed me. She cursed like a roughneck but she laughed like an angel and I learned that she'd had a lot of boyfriends and I kept running into them in bars and at parties and I had to fight them one after another. The last one, a stockcar driver, was the toughest one and I nearly killed him.

Sound: the car pulls and stops.

Wade: There you go, Clayton. It's on the Maxwell's. Welcome home.

Sound: exterior, truck stop. We can hear semi-trailers idling like hungry ogres and traffic on the highway in the deeper distance.

Clayton: *V.O.* I stood outside of the diner where Jodie worked and I suddenly felt rejuvenated. The love we'd had together couldn't have *all* disappeared.

Music from the diner gets closer as he moves toward it.

Clayton: *V.O.* We can rekindle it, I thought, we can make it work again. We can get married and have a kid and the kid will have a way of softening my dad up and he'll stop drinking so much and things will get better between us all. I'll start working at my old friend's body shop and I'll become a regular partner in it and my brother will go to college and learn a good trade and he won't be so introverted anymore and my mother won't be so sad.

Sound: a big truck starts up and shatters the moment.

Clayton: *V.O.* I got right to the door of the diner but instead of going inside I went to a window and I saw her almost immediately and she looked so beautiful I could've cried. She was taking an order and did not see me. There was a pay phone nearby and I decided to phone her instead.

Sound: he enters the phone booth and closes the door, and all the previous sounds are muffled. Coins fall into slot and the phone rings.

Jodie: *Answers.* Hello, Husky. Can I help you?

Sound: music from a jukebox and conversation in the background.

Clayton: Jodie? It's Clayton. I'm home.

Jodie: *A little shocked.* You're kidding.

Clayton: No.

Jodie: Where are you?

Clayton: I'm here, I mean I'm right outside. I'm calling from the pay phone.

Jodie: Why are you doing *that?*

Clayton: I don't know why. Can you take a break?

Jodie: I guess so.

Clayton: Meet me outside by the back door.

Jodie: Okay.

Sound: the idling of semi-trailors is more faint back here behind the diner but the highway is closer, and when the back door opens up the music from within swells for a moment then disappears when the door closes again.

Clayton: *A moment.* You look great, Jodie.

Jodie: When did you get out?

Clayton: Yesterday. I got paroled. How are you?

Jodie: I'm fine...I'm really good.

Clayton: What time do you get off? I got a room for tonight.

Jodie: I only started at six — I'm not done until four or five in the morning. Listen, Clayton...there's something I have to tell you. This is hard so I'll just say it. I'm seeing someone and I guess it's pretty serious.

Clayton: Yeah, I heard. Who is it?

Jodie: We had no idea you'd be getting out so soon — why didn't you phone me first?

Clayton: Who is it, Jodie?

Jodie: It's Bobby Baron. *Beat.*

Clayton: That doesn't make any sense.

Jodie: I was planning to call you.

Clayton: Were you seeing each other the last time we talked?

Jodie: We'd just started to, Clay, I didn't have any idea that it would —

Clayton: Why did he hire me then?

Jodie: Because we *care* about you. Because we wanted to do the right thing.

Clayton: Oh I see what you mean.

Jodie: Don't be sarcastic.

Clayton: *Shouts.* I had a right to know!

Jodie: Don't yell at me!

Clayton: You said you would wait for me!

Jodie: I've changed! I'm not the same person I used to be!

Clayton: What the hell does *that* mean?

Jodie: It means that I'm different now!

Clayton: No, you're no different, Jodie. You're still the same wild slut you always were.

Jodie: You son-of-a-bitch!

Clayton: *Advancing.* Come here.

Jodie: You nearly ruined my life!

Sound: they struggle and hit each other.

Clayton: *V.O.* She starts to go back inside and I grab her and she turns around and she takes another swing at me and I throw her against the building and then I don't know I can't help myself I punch her and she goes down on her knees and I kick her. And then I just leave her there.

Music: under.

Clayton: *V.O.* I had never hit a woman before, let alone a woman I loved, and I was sick to my stomach about it and my head was buzzing like it had flies inside of it. I walked all the way back to the motel on foot and on the road I was assaulted by ghosts from my past and one of them was my father who is a living ghost of flesh and bone, who will not die, who will not die.

Music: strangely.

Jerry: You've made my life miserable, boy.

Clayton: What did I do?

Jerry: Before *you* came along my wife was my woman and we were in love. You must have plotted against us in the womb.

Clayton: How could I do that, dad? I wasn't even born yet.

Jerry: You had a language that only she understood and you turned her against me.

Clayton: That's crazy! You're insane!

Jerry: And all those nights at the kitchen table in your high chair she'd feed you with a spoon like a damned airplane and every time she put food in your mouth you looked at me. You were only a baby but there was badness in your eyes already.

Clayton: A baby doesn't know what's in his eyes.

Jerry: She used to sing me songs.

Clayton: I know.

Jerry: *Sings.*
> Good-night and sweet dreams sung the moon up above,
> to the sailor adrift on the sea.
> He stands alone on the deck of his ship,
> with his heart gone searching for thee.

Clayton: I'm sorry if I made you miserable.

Jerry: A man doesn't expect his children to grow up to be hood-lums and thieves — it's a blow to his ego and a blow to his self-image.

Clayton: Do you forgive me though?

Jerry: I don't know if I can.

Clayton: Why not?

Jerry: Because a man can be too soft in this world and every time he breaks down and forgives another man he loses some of his sinew and a little bit of his bone.

Clayton: I didn't know that.

Jerry: Well it's true.

Clayton: I want to borrow your rifle.

Jerry: Why?

Clayton: Because I want to learn to become a taxidermist and I need to shoot a few things to stuff.

Jerry: I'll tell you what. You take your brother and go out on the highway first and pick up some road kill to practice on and then if you have any natural talent I'll let you borrow the rifle.

Clayton: How will I know if I have any natural talent?

Jerry: I'll be the judge of it.

Clayton: Dad, I know I've been a lousy son but don't take it out on Donovan.

Jerry: *Receding, sings.*

> Good-night and sweet dreams
> sung the moon up above,
> to the sailor adrift on the sea.

Clayton: If you hurt him I'll kill you.

Jerry: *Further.*

> He stands alone on the deck of his ship,
> with his heart gone searching for thee.

Clayton: *Calling; painfully.* I don't forgive you!

Clayton: *V.O.* It took me an hour to get back to the motel and many ghosts assaulted me on the way but none of them were as bony and real as my father. And just as I was putting the key in the door a car drove up behind me.

Sound: a car pulls up and stops.

Clayton: *V.O.* It was Donovan and his girlfriend. They'd run away.

TEN

Sound: interior, motel room, TV on.

Donovan: I climbed out the window of my bedroom.

Tracy: So did I.

Donovan: I pushed your car down the street by hand. It's lucky I've been lifting weights.

Clayton: Jeez, Donovan.

Donovan: We just need somewhere to hide for tonight and then we're going to go to the ocean and live on the beach. We'll go on the bus, I know you want your car back, that's okay. Tracy's never been on a bus before.

Tracy: I've never even been out of the province yet.

Clayton: You're going to get caught.

Donovan: No we won't.

Clayton: Her father's going to track you down.

Tracy: My father belongs in the nuthouse.

Donovan: We'll get on a fishing boat and go to South America and live on an island somewhere and pretty soon they'll even stop looking for us. People disappear all the time. Hell, by then the whole world will be up in flames anyway, everybody will be bombing the crap out of each other.

Clayton: Give me the keys.

Donovan: Where are you going?

Clayton: I'm going to go out and move the car around to the back so nobody will see it.

Donovan: That's a good idea.

Clayton: Don't *do* anything. Just sit there.

Donovan: Okay.

Music: transition.
Sound: car driving.

Clayton: *V.O.* I had no intention of letting them stay overnight with me and I figured I had about an hour to talk them out of it before someone found out and came looking. I was thinking how everything had come down to this moment — how all my life I'd thought the world was a random and haphazard place and how I suddenly knew it wasn't.

Sound: car parking.

Clayton: *V.O.* And I was thinking about the prison that was in my own soul.

ELEVEN

Sound: that inmate gently crying.

Clayton:

> But this is the room I once stood in
> Before the world, or I, ever breathed...

He turns a page.

> Before the sun and the moon were imagined,
> When only shadows fell in through my window.
> This stone wall is the cosmos I dream against
> Or the skullworks I crash my brains against.

Inmate: *Softly.* I want to die now, Clayton.

Clayton: What did you say?

Inmate: I think I want to die now.

Clayton: No, Chief, rage. Don't let them get you down.

Inmate: My wife ran off with another man. She took the kids and the dogs and the truck and she left me with nothing.

Clayton: I know the feeling.

Inmate: You do?

Clayton: More or less. What are you in for anyway? I've never known.

Inmate: I, I killed someone. I didn't mean to.

Clayton: Was it someone you knew?

Inmate: It was my father. But I don't think I knew him very well.

Clayton: I've thought about killing my father a few times but I've always stopped myself.

Inmate: Is he dead now?

Clayton: No, he's still alive.

Inmate: Then maybe you will someday. There's still time for it.

Clayton: Do you like poetry, Chief? I'll read you one from this book I have. This man writes a lot about death. In fact, that's just about all he writes about.

Sound: he flips a few pages.

Clayton: Listen to this one:
> Death is drawn to the foot of my bed,
> A crow with black eyes, blue-billed,
> Soundless as a bone, waiting for the boneless,
> Waiting to fill up the stillness with hisses:
> But listen, there are bells in the spaces
> Between the crow and the shadow of the crow
> Where my last tune is unrung, as a stone unflung,
> As a bone carved into a whistle.
> And death is drawn to the foot of my bed,
> A boat with no admiral, adrift,
> Soundless as a tomb but nameless as a bone,
> And the throats of the bells fill the spaces.

It's a poem about fearing death but it has a positive message too, eh? It's about getting the last drop out of life. Beat. Eh, Chief? About singing one more song before you go. Beat. Chief? Beat. Hey, Chief!

Inmate: I'm still here, Clayton.

Clayton: You scared me.

Inmate: *Laughs.* I'd have to be pretty clever to die that fast. By the way, I'm not a chief. It's Henry.

Clayton: Okay, Henry. See you in the morning.

Inmate: Okay, Clayton.

TWELVE

Music: transition.

Clayton: *V.O.* I had gone to move the car so no one would see it, and I was sitting back there behind the motel, just sitting there, and I had a sudden thought. What if I just drove off? What if I drove toward the mountains and never looked back. All I would lose is my duffle bag and a few clothes and my shaving gear. There was nothing to stop me. To hell with the job! To hell with forgiveness! To hell with my brother — I'm no brother's keeper!

Sound: he revs the car up a few times — then he shuts the engine off.

Clayton: *V.O.* But I couldn't. I just couldn't.

Sound: door opens and closes.

Clayton: *V.O.* So I walked back around to the front of the motel and just as I turned the corner I saw a pick-up truck drive into the parking lot and a man climbed out and he pulled a crowbar out of the box of the truck and he went directly to the door of my room. It was Bobby Baron and he didn't look happy.

Sound: in the near distance the man bangs on the door with his crowbar.

Bobby: Open the door, you son-of-a-bitch!

Clayton: *V.O.* No, he didn't look happy at all.

Bobby: I'll break it in!

Clayton: *V.O.* Well, I didn't have any choice, did I. It'd all come to this. I would take my beating like a man and face the new day if I lived. I started toward him and I was just about to call out his name when a shot rang out.

Sound: a shot comes through the door.

Clayton: *V.O.* It rips through the door from inside and the bullet strikes Bobby in the chest and he staggers and the crowbar drops from his hand and he falls against the front of his truck and then he slumps onto the pavement.

Music: sting.

Clayton: *V.O.* I run to the door and stand to the side of it.

Clayton: Donovan! It's me! Open up!

Clayton: *V.O.* And he opens the door and he's standing there with the Browning 9 mm in his hand. His eyes are wild with adrenaline and his girlfriend is hiding behind the bed and her eyes are wild too.

Clayton: Give me the gun!

Donovan: We thought it was Tracy's father! He scared the hell out of us!

Clayton: Take the car keys! It's behind the motel!

Donovan: Where should I go?

Clayton: Take Tracy home, then *you* go home, and don't wake anyone up! Hurry!

Donovan: What're you going to do?

Clayton: Donovan, just do what I say. Get going!

Donovan: *To Tracy.* Come on! Hurry up!

Tracy: *Approaching.* Who is it? Did you kill him? Oh my god! *And she begins to scream.*

Clayton: Get going!

Music: transition.

Clayton: *V.O.* They disappeared around the corner of the motel and I went over to Bobby.

Clayton: Hey, Bobby, can you hear me?

Sound: sirens.

Clayton: *V.O.* The bullet had entered him right below his heart and between his lungs. It had lodged against his spine but didn't even scratch it.

Policeman: *Approaching.* Put the gun down! Put it down!

Clayton: *V.O.* He had surgery to remove the slug and spent a few weeks in the hospital. It was rumoured he would never walk again but that was just a story — he walked out of the hospital and into Jodie's arms.

Policeman: Did you shoot that man?

Clayton: Yes, sir.

Policeman: Lay down on the pavement and put your hands behind your back. Do it *now*!

Clayton: I'm doing it, sir.

Clayton: *V.O.* And I found out much later that Donovan had tried to kill himself that very same spring by putting a garden hose into my car from the exhaust system but had failed when the hose fell off.

Sound: the click of cuffs.

Policeman: *Into his radio.* 4-42. I need a medic fast!

Dispatch: *Almost inaudible.* On it's way, 4-42.

Clayton: *V.O.* And I found out much later that my mother had been hooked on codeine for her headaches since I'd been a boy of eleven or twelve and the codeine had finally ruined her heart.

Policeman: Who are you?

Clayton: Clayton Sydora.

Policeman: Are you alone?

Clayton: Yes, sir. I'm all alone.

Clayton: *V.O.* And I found out much later that I had *always* been alone and that being alone was normal for me.

Sound: another set of sirens approaches.

Policeman: Why did you shoot him?

Clayton: Because he attacked me with a crowbar, sir. I was defending myself.

Music transition.

THIRTEEN

Clayton: *V.O.* But the judge didn't see it that way. I was sentenced to seven years without parole for possession of an illicit firearm and assault with intent.

Sound: auto-gate slides open.

Prison official: Welcome back, Clayton.

Clayton: Hello, boys.

Prison official: *Over his shoulder.* One for detainment!

Sound: auto-gate closes with a solid thud.

Clayton: *V.O.* The gun was traced to a rancher in Saskatchewan who had reported it stolen. I told the police I had found it by the side of the road while I was hitchhiking and nobody could prove otherwise. The car with the Manitoba licence plates never re-entered the picture, nor did the man who I left on his belly by the side of the road, nor did the man with the brand-new hole in his head who I left by a creek in the Clearwater Hills. The coyotes and the weasels and the crows and the hawks would've taken care of him.

Music under.

Clayton: *V.O.* I went back to prison and in the spring of the following year my mother died of a heart attack and Donovan left home for good. He has phoned me from time to time from various places around the country since then and he has sent me things in the mail, mostly books because he knows I like them, and now this postcard from Tofino by the sea where he says that he is happy.

I have not seen my father or even heard from him since my mother's funeral, which I was allowed to go to under guard. He still lives in the house I grew up in but he doesn't work anymore. People say he's gone crazy and I say he always was.

Sound: visitors' room, a chair slides as someone sits. Bits of conversation and a game of ping-pong in the background.

Trevor: How are you doing, Clayton?

Clayton: I'm okay. How are you?

Trevor: Oh, I've been better. One of my boys stepped in front of the c-train yesterday.

Clayton: Sorry to hear that, Trevor.

Trevor: He was only your brother's age.

Clayton: That's tough.

Trevor: Clayton, I went through your court transcripts again —

Clayton: You're wasting your time.

Trevor: I still don't believe you shot him, son.

Clayton: Well it doesn't much matter what you believe, does it.

Trevor: When I was your age I was involved in a lot bad things… I was lost and afraid…my good judgement clouded by drugs and booze and anger and I felt friggin' *worthless*…damnit, Clayton…the world is hard enough as it is —

Clayton: What're you trying to say?

Trevor: It hurts me to see you like this! *Beat.* I have to go.

Clayton: You'll be back. Won't you?

Trevor: Yeah… *Softens.* I'll be back.

Sound: that inmate sings, as if from a bottom of a well, heartfelt.

Clayton: *V.O.* So my life has become simplified. My thoughts go round and round and so do the voices in my head and the sound of the sea that is in my imagination rolls on and on and my hopes and my dreams move in and out of the mist like grey wolves with mysterious eyes.

Old guard: *Distant.* Quiet in the block!

Clayton: *V.O.* My brother is safe and I'm finding some peace with myself. A day at a time.

Old guard: *Closer.* Lights out!

Clayton: *V.O.*

> And my heart will not dash on the rocks
> Nor will it stop teaching me, crying:

Oh wind, oh tumultuous sea! Hurl me
Again and again, for I've not learned my verses yet,
And the waves still want me.

Old guard: *Close by.* Go to sleep now, Clayton. That's a good boy.

Sound: the guard walks away and the inmate sings on and on...
Music out.

END

METASTASIS

A TRAGICOMEDY IN TWO ACTS

Christine Hanson as EuLaLa, Glen Gaston as Hardball, and John B. Lowe as Deerborn.
(Ed Ellis, University of Alberta Archives)

METASTASIS was first performed by Northern Light Theatre in Edmonton from October 17–29, 1995, under the direction of D.D. Kugler with the following cast:

Kenny/Sebastion/Waiter: Damien Atkins*
Deerborn/Biker/Bartender: John B. Lowe*
McCoo/Therapist/Thorpe: Glen Nelson*
Carol/Helen: Sandra Nicholls*
Tammy/Tiger/Alice: Kerry Ann Doherty
Trudy/Maria/Hooker: Pamela Finlayson
Hardball/Healey/Dr. Doc Holiday: Glen Gaston*
Cellist/EuLaLa: Christine Hanson
Howie/Wade/Shep: Jimmie Hodges
* Member of Actors Equity

PRODUCTION
Artistic Associate: Jonathan Christenson
Costume: Dave Boechler
Set and Lighting: Melinda Sutton
Sound: Darrin Hagen
Stage Manager: Susan Hayes

Metastasis was subsequently produced at the Montreal Fringe Festival in 1998 and by the Company of Rogues in Calgary in 1999. It won the 1994 Alberta Playwrights' Network Annual Playwriting Competition (Full-Length Category), followed by a summer workshop at the Page-to-Stage Festival at the National Arts Centre in Ottawa.

CHARACTERS
MULTICAST IF DESIRED AS BELOW:
Kenny McCoo, Sebastion Deerborn, Waiter
Martin Deerborn, Biker, Bartender
Therapist, Ken McCoo, Horatio Thorpe
Carol Deerborn, Helen McCoo
Tammy, Tiger, Alice McCoo
Trudy, Maria, Hooker
Hardball, Healey, Dr. Doc Holiday, Jogger
A female cellist
Howie McCoo, Wade, Shep

STAGING

The play takes place in a ruined domicile of indeterminate size, age, and rank in society. Whatever the story it's a woeful one: something has flung the house down. A bomb, a tornado, the Wrath of God...

People from several walks of life share the space, most of who never meet; this "house" holds a multiple of realities woven together.

The style is open and minimal and somewhat unnatural. For instance, the car in the last scene might be a piece of frame, a steering wheel, a front seat, a brake drum or two. It might be strewn where the driveway once was or up in a ravaged tree. Things have been upheaved. There might be an entrance through an earthquake's crack in the stage. Wade's sculpture might be made of debris from the fallen house.

When the actors and actresses aren't performing in their speaking parts, they might appear as crowd or passersby or witnesses moving about in the playing space. There are no specific stage directions for this. It would be the director's call.

The cellist is omnipresent and invisible to others except in one scene where she appears as the character EuLaLa. She's sort of angelic, if slightly besmirched, dirty-faced, smudges on her knees, and she wears a tattered white dress. A wobbly halo above her head wouldn't be out of place. She plays cello as a transition device between scenes and to underscore certain passages at the discretion of the director.

ONE

Hardball, at this point just a voice and a shadow on the wall, wears a baseball cap, long coat, cigarette in his mouth. Deerborn's shirt is half undone and his suspenders dangle. Tammy, in a nurse's uniform, has her panties in her hand and her arms around Deerborn. They are kissing goodnight in a doorway.

Hardball: *V.O.* You don't know me, Dr. Deerborn. We haven't been introduced to each other yet. But soon enough.

Tammy: *Breathlessly.* G'night, Doctor.

Deerborn: Sweet dreams, Nurse.

Tammy: Of you. *She holds her panties up to her face like a veil and slips out the door with a little laugh.*

Hardball: *V.O.* I'm dying to get to know you, Dr. Deerborn.

Deerborn closes the door and leans against it.

At first you won't open up to me but gradually the door of your cage will loosen and you will open yourself wider and wider until you have all of me. Then we'll play some hardball. *Whispers.* Dr. Deerborn?

Deerborn: Is somebody there? *He opens the door and looks.*

Nothing.

TWO

Carol: *Her bedside phone rings.* Hello?

Deerborn: Did I wake you up?

Carol: I'm reading in bed.

Deerborn: That sounds cozy.

Carol: Where are you?

Deerborn: I'm calling from the car, the traffic is terrible. Don't wait up for me.

Carol: I've barely seen you all week.

Deerborn: It's been one of those weeks.

Carol: Maybe I *want* to wait up.

Deerborn: Really, Carol, don't. I'm completely done in tonight, and I'm grouchy and I'm…you know. *He smells his hand.*

Carol: You missed dinner.

Deerborn: Didn't I tell you I had to stay late?

Carol: No.

Deerborn: I thought I did.

Carol: I made Italian.

Deerborn: Darnit! I'm sorry.

Carol: *Sexy.* Guess where my hand is right now. *Pause.* Martin, guess where my hand is right now. *Pause.* Are you still there, Martin?

Deerborn: Go back to your book, Carol. I'll talk to you in the morning. G'night.

Carol: Sure. *They hang up.* In the morning. *Carol tosses her book away and turns out the bedside lamp. A moment in darkness.*

Hardball: *V.O.* Gently…gently open. Push!

Then two loud blasts from a shotgun which ripple for several seconds after. The shots should shake the theatre.

Hardball: *V.O.* It's begun.

THREE

Dr. Doc Holiday: *In bloodspeckled greens and a cowboy hat. Cheerful.* Over here, Mrs. Deerborn!

Carol: *Approaching quickly.* Where's my husband?

Dr. Doc Holiday: He's gonna be okay, Mrs. Deerborn, you can take him right on home. He's a very lucky man though.

Carol: Thank God.

Dr. Doc Holiday: I'm Dr. Doc Holiday. We met at the last Christmas party. I was playin' the piano.

Carol: Can I see him?

Dr. Doc Holiday: He's with a policeman — shouldn't be another minute.

Carol: Why the police? What do you mean?

Dr. Doc Holiday: What've you been told?

Carol: I was told he drove off the road.

Dr. Doc Holiday: Oh. Maybe you better sit down.

Carol: Out with it!

Dr. Doc Holiday: Somebody took a potshot at him on the freeway, Mrs. Deerborn.... Commonly known as a drive-by shooting. He wasn't hit, and that was good, it being a sawed-off shotgun, ma'am, but he's got a few bumps and bruises...

Carol: Get out of my way!

Dr. Doc Holiday: Straight through there.

FOUR

Carol: Here, darling.

She gives him a painkiller. Deerborn has his arm in a sling and a large bandage in the middle of his forehead.

Deerborn: Thank you. It's good to be home.

Carol: Can I get you something else while I'm up?

Deerborn: No. Come sit by me.

Carol: *Sitting on the sofa with him.* Oh Marty...*why?* Why you? What's the matter with this world?

Deerborn: It's the work of the Devil, it's become deranged.

Carol: You could've been... *Bites her knuckle.*

Deerborn: Go ahead and say it, Carol. I could've been *killed.* Shot in the head. My brains all over the —

Carol: Be quiet.

Deerborn: Upholstery.

Carol: Hush.

Deerborn: If I'd *just* come home for dinner none of this would've...

Carol: Ssshh. No, hush.

Deerborn: I feel terrible. The Mercedes was only two weeks old and now it's full of little holes.

Carol: The Mercedes can be fixed. *She puts her head on his shoulder.*

Deerborn: Ow!

Carol: Sore shoulder?

Deerborn: Yes!

Carol: I'll have Maria make up the spare room for you, darling, you'll sleep better alone for a night or two.

Deerborn: I don't like the spare room.

Carol: Then Sebastion's old room.

Deerborn: I don't like that room either, I might not ever sleep again. *She strokes his hair.* Carol, I saw the eyes of the one with the shotgun, I saw them aiming down the barrel at me. He looked so young...he was wearing a ski mask.

Carol: He's an animal.

Deerborn: I'll never forget those eyes.

Carol: Oh Marty...

Deerborn: And it's true what they say: my whole life flashed through my mind. I saw myself at different angles and ages like flipping through a photo album, and I think I saw the face of God. He looked like my old Aunt Izzy.

Carol: The one who left you her cello.

Deerborn: The spooky old hag, she's come back to haunt me.

Carol: You've been traumatized, darling, it's going to take some time.

Deerborn: I guess so.

Carol: Sleep now? Somewhere?

Deerborn: *Sighs deeply.* I'll try to.

FIVE

Maria: *Gently.* Good morning, Dr. Deerborn.

Deerborn: *Downcast.* Good morning, Maria.

Maria: I hope you are feeling much better today. Such an awful thing.

Deerborn: I feel lousy. My head is banging.

Maria: You sit there, I will bring you some coffee and the paper is there and I'm making your favourite omelette, the old Spanish one from my grandmother's book. You like that one.

Deerborn: Where's Mrs. Deerborn this morning?

Maria: She went to see her friend today.

Deerborn: You mean her shrink. *He sips his coffee.* The coffee tastes funny. What did you do to it, Maria?

Maria: It's the same as I always make it, Doctor.

Deerborn: It tastes funny.

The telephone rings.

Maria: *Answering.* Deerborn residence. *Pause.* Can I ask who is this calling please? *Pause.* One moment please. *Then to him.* Dr. Deerborn, a young woman, she says her name is Tammy, don't talk unless you want to. I'll say you're still in bed.

Deerborn: *Beat.* I'll take it.

Maria: You don't have to if you...

Deerborn: Give me the phone and leave me by myself.

Maria: *Si*, Dr. Deerborn.

Deerborn: English, Maria.

Maria: Sorry, Dr. Deerborn...whenever I make that crazy omelette... *She exits.*

Lights up on Tammy.

Deerborn: *Quietly.* I told you never to call me here.

Tammy: *On the edge of tears.* I had to!

Deerborn: Don't make a scene, Tammy.

Tammy: My poor, poor baby!

Deerborn: I'm alive, they missed me.

Tammy: Who did?

Deerborn: What do you mean *who?* How the hell should I know WHO!

Tammy: *Short.* Oh.

Deerborn: Do you think I KNOW who did it? Do you think there's somebody GUNNING for me, somebody's HIT MAN!

Tammy: *Quietly.* Well you had that malpractice suit last month...

Deerborn: Thanks for phoning, Tammy, you've really made my day.

Tammy: Martin, I'm just —

Deerborn: Nothing ever happened between us, got that? No more goo-goo eyes, no more footsy tag! If you so much as *glance* at me again I'll have your stripes!

Tammy: Martin — *He hangs up on her.* Wow.

Dr. Doc Holiday: *Approaches with clipboard; more blood on his tunic.* You look like your dawg died, Nurse.

Tammy: Don't drawl in my face, Holiday.

Dr. Doc Holiday: Whatsa matter?

Tammy: Married men are so weird.

Dr. Doc Holiday: I've got two tickets to a piano and cello concerto tonight. Champagne, smoked salmon, snooty conversation...

Tammy: I don't think so.

Dr. Doc Holiday: How 'bout some lunch?

Tammy: I'm busy for lunch.

Dr. Doc Holiday: How 'bout some flippy-flop? You name the place.

Tammy: Yeh yeh.

Dr. Doc Holiday: Just get a new dawg.

Tammy: Sure. Simple.

He walks away whistling the theme to High Noon. *Tammy smacks herself in the head.*

I *love* smoked salmon!

SIX

IN A FANCY RESTAURANT

Trudy: Serves you right.

Tammy: What do you mean?

Trudy: Oh, stop pretending.

Tammy: Be nice to me, Trudy, I'm wounded.

Trudy: I love you like a sister, Tammy, but you're stupid to think that a man like him could really care for a girl like you. To put it bluntly, you are, to men like him, as common as dirt is.

Tammy: I've heard this all before.

Trudy: Under their feet.

Tammy: You're just jealous.

Trudy: Here we go.

Tammy: You've *always* been jealous of me.

Trudy: This is going to get ugly.

Tammy: Ever since high school, all of my boyfriends, you always drooled over them like some kind of —

Trudy: Ever since grade *six* you've always gone after the richest guys and then you act so *smug* about it.

Tammy: I can't help it if classy men find me attractive.

Trudy: Does LOVE ever enter the picture?

Tammy: Sure. I love nice clothes, fancy restaurants, airplane tickets, hot sex...

Trudy: You're shameless.

Tammy: Don't preach to me about love! You don't *love* men, you just wanna *save* them all like some kind of salvation army daughter, just like you're doing with whatshisname, that guy you've been bonking, that *biker* with the big forehead.

Trudy: Healey.

Tammy: He was in jail once, right?

Trudy: A *while* ago.

Tammy: You sure know how to pick them, Trudy, a biker with a record with one eyebrow. Gets *me* all wet.

Trudy: He's a motorcycle mechanic.

Tammy: Oo! And that's why you dropped out of nursing school and became a barmaid so you could hump a greaseball.

Trudy: So what's so big about being a nurse?

Tammy: The doctors are.

Trudy: You mean *were*.

Tammy: There's more where that one came from.

Trudy: Psycho tart strikes again.

Tammy: Call me names. That's your style. While you and your little family of grim reapers are finding homey contentment in the lower-middle class, me and this built-for-fun body I'm in will be living in a big house with a swimming pool in Upper Mount Royal.

Trudy: You and that "built-for-fun" body you're in are both a couple of cheap sluts.

Tammy: *Quietly folds her napkin.* I'm moving out of our apartment, Trudy. I've been thinking about this for quite a bit longer than you might suspect and I've had it up to HERE with you. You're bitchy and petty and *jealous* and —

Trudy: Good luck with your life.

Tammy: Good riddance. *She exits.*

Trudy: Tammy...?! *Big sigh.*

Waiter: *Approaches.* Could I...interest you in something else, Mademoiselle?

Trudy: Yeh. A smaller mouth and a new set of brains.

Waiter: We have some beautiful sweetbreads.

Trudy: *Looks at him.* What?

Waiter: Sweetbreads.

SEVEN

Two men gazing down at a motorcycle.

Biker: Diaphragm?

Healey: Something like that.

Biker: Rocker arm.

Healey: Link arm.

Biker: Maybe it's just a seal or a spring.

Healey: Gasket?

Biker: Air jet?

Healey: Acceleration pump.

Biker: Emulsion block.

Healey: One of those.

Biker: Yup.

Healey: Y'want me to pull it apart and have a look?

Biker: When could you?

Healey: *Glances around the shop. Checks his watch.* Sometime this afternoon?

Biker: Sounds good, man. I'd do it myself, eh, but ever since I chopped these fingers off I can't get into those littler places anymore.

Healey: Wounds *make* the man, don't ever forget.

Biker: I hear ya. *Trudy enters.* I'll go watch some pool down at my brother's clubhouse. Maybe you could give me a call down there after you get it pulled apart. How'd that be?

Healey: Perfect. *To Trudy. Tentative.* Hi there.

Trudy: *Same.* Hi.

Healey: I heard your brother got the crap beat out of him the other night.

Biker: Yeh. *Laughs.* Some guy who looks like Boris Karloff worked him over with a big metal chair. Same guy who pounded him out at the picnic last summer.

Healey: Oops.

Biker: That's what I said.

Healey: *To Trudy.* He'll probably hire some guy from Montana to come up and shoot the guy now.

Biker: That's ex*act*ly what I said. *To Trudy.* You can beat up my brother once but if you beat him up twice he'll probably hire some guy from Montana to come up and shoot you.

Healey: There's some kind of lesson in this.

Biker: Violence is a good teacher. *Both laugh.* Okay, Healey, just call me down at my brother's clubhouse and that's where I'll be.

Healey: Okay, Stuart, I'll call you there, man.

Biker: …It's Steven. My brother is Stuart.

Healey: OH! Shit! I always get you two guys mixed up. *To Trudy.* They look so much alike y'know and they both ride the same kind of bikes and they both have body parts missing in action... *Biker nods, shows missing finger.*

Biker: I'm thinking I should shave my beard off or grow my hair or something. Stuart is earning a lot of enemies lately.

Healey: Maybe you should buy a horse and get out of Dodge. *He laughs but Biker doesn't.*

Biker: What do you mean?

Healey: It's a joke.

Biker: *Beat.* OH! *They both laugh hard.* Okay, man. *Snaps his fingers.* Later.

Healey: Talk to ya later, man.

Biker: Nice meeting you.

Healey: That's Trudy. You met her at the picnic.

Biker: Did I? Oh yeh! How's it goin'?

Trudy: It's fine.

Biker: *Laughing...*get out of Dodge. *Exits.*

Trudy: He's pretty funny.

Healey: His brother's even funnier. *He goes to work on the bike.*

Trudy: Healey...I came by to say I'm sorry for last night how I flew off the handle at you. I feel really bad about it.

Healey: I called you at noontime but nobody answered.

Trudy: Did you leave me a message?

Healey: It wasn't very big. ·

Trudy: I was having lunch with Tammy.

Healey: How's Tammy?

Trudy: That's sort of the other reason why I'm here.

Healey: Why's that?

Trudy: First tell me what the message was you left me.

Healey: *Stops working.* I said I didn't mean to say everything

I said last night either. I said I was being a jerk. And I said I'm sorry about that hole in your wall and I'll patch it up after shop today.

Trudy: Those were nice things to say, Healey.

Healey: I hate answering machines.

Trudy: I'd pretty much decided we'd broken up.

Healey: Yeh. So did I.

Trudy: I thought that was *it* for us.

Healey: Me too.

Trudy: Kaputski!

Healey: So if you didn't get my message what made you come over here then?

Trudy: I dunno, the whole dumb day, stuff with Tammy...

Healey: So what's this stuff about Tammy? *He starts working again.*

Trudy: We had a big fight in the restaurant.

Healey: Food fight?

Trudy: Pretty close to one.

Healey: What about?

Trudy: The doctor dumped her.

Healey: Big news.

Trudy: That's what I said.

Healey: She's crazy to think that guys like him really care for girls like her.

Trudy: That's *exactly* what I said, and when I wouldn't let her cry on my shoulder about it we started arguing like a couple of lunatics. She said she was moving out of our apartment and then she sashayed out of there.

Healey: Doing the rumbabumba.

Trudy: It's been coming for a long time.

Glen Gaston as Healey and Pamela Finlayson as Trudy.
(Ed Ellis, University of Alberta Archives)

Healey: No big surprise.

Trudy: Damnit, Healey, we'd been attached at the hip since grade six. We had the same clothes and the same hair until we were seventeen, we both left town to go to nursing school together, we both lost our virginity to the same quarterback...

Healey: *Stops working.* At the same time?

Trudy: No. Same weekend though. And it's taken me the whole next decade to realize we're just plain sick of each other.

Healey: When's she moving out?

Trudy: As we speak.

Healey: *Adios.*

Trudy: Which brings me to the question of what I'm going to do for a roommate since I can't afford to live there alone and all the quarterbacks are already taken.

Healey: *Beat. Ohh nooo...!*

Trudy: Honey, listen to me, and don't get your shirt in a knot, you've been living like a hermit for far too long.

Healey: There's things about me you don't want to dwell under the same roof with, Trudy.

Trudy: Healey...awwww... *Cuddling up to him.*

Healey: No! And that's final.

EIGHT

Tiger: Hi, Kenny.

Kenny: *Smoking, leaning against a wall.* Hi, Tiger.

Tiger: I haven't seen you around for a while, how's the summer going?

Kenny: It's going.

Tiger: Bum a smoke? *He gives her one from his pack.* Are you joining up for track-and-field again?

Kenny: I don't know. Are you? *Lights her smoke.*

Tiger: No. My interests are changing. I guess I should tell you this, Kenny, I met this other guy. His name is Shep, short for Shepard. I think you'd like him though, he's really cool. He quit school and he owns his own car.

Kenny: Kurt Cobain died.

Tiger: Really? When?

Kenny: Just now. Today. He shot himself.

Tiger: Wow. *Pause.* Would ya like to go out with Shep and me somewhere? Just drive around, I don't know. I mean can't we all be friends for a while, I mean none of us have had sex with each other yet.

Kenny: *Shrugs.* I'll think about it.

Tiger: His father's in the peace-keeping forces somewhere.

Kenny: Oh yeh?

Tiger: Just call me sometime.

Kenny: I might.

NINE

Therapist: I haven't seen you for a month, Carol. What's going on?

Carol: *Wiping tears away.* I don't know where to start. *Yanks out a Kleenex and blows her nose.*

Therapist: We've known each other for a long time, you know you can tell me anything. Start at the top. Be brave.

Carol: Well...after the drive-by shooting...Martin began acting so strange.

Therapist: How?

Carol: *Strangely.* ...I don't know...not himself, not the man I married — the kind man, the man content with his life... the loving man.

Therapist: What did he become?

Carol: *Un*kind. *Dis*content. Mean-spirited and suspicious and...

Therapist: *Un*loving?

Carol: Yes.

Therapist: You feel unloved.

Carol: Yes. And he fired the maid for no good reason and he locked up his cello in the basement. He's gotten so paranoid.

Therapist: Has he gone back to work?

Carol: He *tried* to.

Therapist: What happened?

Carol: Oh brother...

A beeping noise from some kind of monitor or machine fades up and into the next scene.

TEN

Deerborn: What does that look like to you, Holiday?

Dr. Doc Holiday: *Happily covered in blood.* Diaphragm?

Deerborn: Nurse...?

Tammy: *Cold.* Yes, Doctor?

Deerborn: Swab that.

Tammy: Where?

Deerborn: All over in there, I can't see a damn thing for the blood. On the double!

Tammy: *Clicks her heels.* Yes, SIR!

Deerborn: And keep your attitude to yourself.

Tammy: What attitude, sir?

Deerborn: Swab! *She does.* What the hell am I supposed to be looking for in here anyway?

Dr. Doc Holiday: Some kind of lump, a tumour.

Deerborn: Where?

Dr. Doc Holiday: What's that?

Deerborn: Poke it with something.

Dr. Doc Holiday: Nurse...?

Tammy: *Sweetly.* Yes, Doctor?

Dr. Doc Holiday: Give me something to poke that with.

Tammy: *More sweetly.* Certainly, Doctor. How's this little thingy? *They play a little game of tug 'n war with the implement.*

Deerborn: Poke it!

Dr. Doc Holiday: Right. *He does.* Hmm.

Deerborn: Is it hard or soft?

Dr. Doc Holiday: Compared to what?

Deerborn: Is it harder than a boiled egg or softer than a boiled egg?

Dr. Doc Holiday: Would that be a *hard*-boiled egg or a *soft*-boiled egg?

Deerborn: Give me that thing!

Dr. Doc Holiday: 'tsall yours.

Tammy: *Smartassed.* Should I *swab* it, Doctor?

Deerborn: Get your paws...! *He slaps her hand.*

Tammy: I was just...

Deerborn: Shut up! *Beat.* Are you bouncing her, Holiday?

Dr. Doc Holiday: Am I *what*?

Deerborn: You heard me. Are you bouncing that nurse?

Dr. Doc Holiday: I don't think that's any of your damn business, Doctor.

Deerborn: You *are* bouncing her!

Dr. Doc Holiday: Just because *you* did doesn't mean nobody else can.

Tammy: Please don't fight over me!

Deerborn: Do you like your residency at this here establishment, you little sonofabitch?

Dr. Doc Holiday: No, sir, I hate it.

Tammy: Don't let him bully you, Doc-Doc.

Dr. Doc Holiday: Don't worry, Tam-Tam.

Deerborn: No first names!

Dr. Doc Holiday: He's losing it.

Deerborn: There'll be no first names in this man's surgery!

Tammy: He's going to poke somebody with that.

Dr. Doc Holiday: Give me that thing, Doctor.

Deerborn: *Breathing heavily.* Why? What's the matter? Why is everybody staring at me? I'm...I'm okay. I'm fine, I'm okay.

Dr. Doc Holiday: Dr. Deerborn...

Deerborn: I said I'm fine!

Dr. Doc Holiday: I'll finish up here, sir — you go relax. Have a coffee. Unwind. Go home. Go to Arizona. *Holiday holds out his hand and Deerborn surrenders the implement.* Thank you, sir.

Deerborn: *Beat.* Carry on, troopers. *He exits.*

Dr. Doc Holiday: Guess who's been working overtime in the old banana factory.

Tammy: The gall of that man!

Dr. Doc Holiday: Give me a kiss. *They kiss.* Gimme a little feel.

Tammy: Not over an open body, Doc.

Dr. Doc Holiday: Who is this anyway? What's it say there?

Tammy: *Reads from her ankle bracelet.* Um... *McCoo, Helen, Mrs.*

Dr. Doc Holiday: Well *McCoo Helen Mrs....* What can we do for you today? *Rubs his hands together.*

Tammy: *Points.* What's that?

Dr. Doc Holiday: That doesn't look good. Does it?

Tammy: It doesn't look good to me.

Dr. Doc Holiday: Let's take it out of 'er then.

Tammy: Do it, Doctor!

Dr. Doc Holiday: Make my day! *Pumps his fist. Tammy squeals.*

The beeping noise fades.

ELEVEN

Carol: After that episode in surgery, administration stepped in and put him on rest leave. He's a very proud man and an excellent surgeon...

Therapist: How did he handle it?

Carol: Oddly.

Therapist: What do you mean?

Carol: Like a little kid home from school with a sore throat. He played with his train set. He coloured. He built a big fort in the living room with some blankets between the sofa and the kitchen chairs.

Therapist: A form of denial, I've seen it before.

Carol: The big fort?

Therapist: Everything, the whole condition. A retreat into the sanctuary of one's childhood past as a way of avoiding one's adulthood, the demanding and terrible present. Isn't uncommon. *He writes something down in his pad.* Then what happened?

Carol: Our son Sebastion phoned from Morocco.

Therapist: Mm-hm?

Carol: He's been abroad on an arts grant this past little while... he was having such a wonderful time over there I couldn't find the words, I didn't know how to break the news to him...

Therapist: Nature's way. Shelter the offspring.

Carol: Not that he'd come rushing home anyway.

Therapist: He wouldn't have?

Carol: He and his father...they have a few *knots* to undo.

Therapist: And *you* and your son are still very close, are you not?

Carol: He's very...attached to me, yes.

Therapist: *Leans forward.* Mm-*hm*?

Carol: *Avoids this.* Well! Then Martin, he, he started to fade away inside himself, slowly by degrees. He moped around the house in his boxer shorts, he slept curled up on the front-room floor like the family dog, he *whined* at night. I didn't know what he needed. I felt something was going to cave in very soon.

Therapist: And did it cave in?

Carol: Oh baby!

Therapist: Get it all out.

TWELVE

Deerborn whines softly and paws at her leg.

Carol: *Lowers her book.* What is it, Marty? Speak, darling. *Say* something. Would you like to go outside?

Deerborn: I have to come to grips with some things.

Carol: I'm listening, dear.

Deerborn: I have to come clean, I...I can't live with myself any longer.

Carol: Is this some kind of confession?

Deerborn: *Nods.* I guess so.

Carol: Sit up. *He does.* Well...? I'm ready.

He takes a deep breath.

Deerborn: I've come to believe in my just desserts. I don't know, maybe there *is* a God, and maybe this God dishes out retribution by manipulating certain events...

Carol: Get to the point, Martin.

Deerborn: Yes. *Clears his throat.* I believe I was shot at that night because of my wanton behaviour.

Carol: That malpractice suit?

Deerborn: No, Carol, *not* that malpractice suit. That malpractice suit *pales* compared to this, this is important, momentous, tragic, kinda sticky... *Unconsciously smells his hand.*

Carol: *Grabs his ear.* I want to know *who* and I want to know *now*.

Deerborn: *Ow! Ow! Ow!*

Carol: Tell me or I'll rip it off.

Deerborn: *A nurse! A nurse! Tammy!*

Carol: *Twists harder.* Which one is that?

Deerborn: At the Christmas party...the one who was singing...!

Carol: You mean the one who was trying to stick the big piano up her little dress.

Deerborn: Yes! *She lets go. He rubs his ear.*

Carol: Why, Martin? In God's name *why*?

Deerborn: *Shrugs.* Stress, release, excitement, danger, detachment...fear of impotency, fear of death. How do I know why?

Carol: How many others?

Deerborn: Nurses?

Carol: Oh Jesus... *She cups her hands between her legs and caves in around herself.*

Deerborn: Yeh I know. I'm a dirty rotten scumbag. But I'm a dirty rotten scumbag who wants another chance. I'm fifty-five years old and I want the rest of my life to be different: clean and chaste and with you. I want to be forgiven.

Carol: I forgive you.

Deerborn: Do you?

Carol: Yes. In an abstract sort of way. Now go pack your bags and get the hell out of my life.

THIRTEEN

Carol: At one point, while he was packing up, I had a fit of con-science and I tried to take my anger back. He hadn't been well, perhaps I was being selfish, too hasty, I mean how would I feel if he jumped off a bridge or lay down in front of a train or blew his brains all out or something. I told him we could talk, I said don't go tonight, perhaps in the light of day...

Therapist: And with what did he respond?

Carol: With nothing. He went right out the door and into the dark and was gone. Laughing. It chilled me to the bone; it didn't sound like the way he laughs, it sounded like somebody else's laughter inside of him.

Therapist: Trauma, Carol, is extremely complex.

Carol: He's staying in a hotel by the tracks. Not a nice hotel either, a real *seedy* one, The Sandman. He LOVES nice hotels. And he took his GUN when he left.

Therapist: This doesn't bode well.

Carol: No.

Therapist: But you're still in touch.

Carol: No, not really, I...I hired a private detective to find him, watch over him. Oh *God*...this whole thing has gotten so out of control, I think I'm losing my mind. So much has happened in such a short time, I...

Therapist: I know you too well, my friend, you're leading me somewhere.

Carol: Am I?

Therapist: *La*dybug…

Carol: Yes. Yes, there *is* something else. I've started seeing someone else already. This embarrasses me a little. Should it?

Therapist: Let it all hang out.

Carol: Well he's twenty-four years younger than me: that makes
him twenty-five but who the hell's counting. He's a sculptor, a metal sculptor, I think he's even quite talented. Short
of conversation but coachable in bed. Am I blushing?

Therapist: Do you love him?

Carol: *Laughs.* I sure as hell hope not.

Therapist: You seem quite pleased with yourself.

Carol: I'm hysterical! My husband is playing with his gun in a
squalid hotel room on the wrong side of the tracks and I'm
having a sexual reawakening with someone half my age,
a bender of metal no less!

Therapist: I couldn't have said it better myself.

Carol: There's more.

Therapist: You know you can tell me anything.

Carol: My sculptor, his name is Wade, he went to art college
with Sebastion. They've been sharing a flat together.
They're best buddies.

Therapist: You're a bad little catfish.

Carol: I ran out of Prozac.

Therapist: Talk dirty to me.

They both break up.

FOURTEEN

Healey: *To a bartender who wears a big head of some kind — a wolf,
a bear.* Everybody called him Szabo but I just called him
The Weasel. When I was a kid he treated me like scum
so why I ever figured it'd be any different as a grown-up

is just my own stupidity. You know what he got me to do with him? Hold up a gas station. With real guns. It was just as you get into dinosaur country right on the highway surrounded by hoodoos and cactus and sagebrush, this Esso. And just before we did it I saw this herd of antelopes, and there was something so beautiful about them, the way they all flowed together in one easy pattern like a pure single thought, like all of God's natural goodness moving me to the clear and I heard myself say to myself *don't do this you dumb piece of shit.* But did I heed? I didn't. And we got caught. And we went to prison, The Weasel and me. And he treated me like scum in there too, always trying to get me to do things for him. Do this, do that. And every friend I ever tried to make in there he somehow put a wedge between us and wedged us apart. He needed a sucker all to himself that he could tell his stupid stories to and to demoralize and to spread his insanity to. And that poor sucker was me. Well. Szabo is dead now and I'm a hotshot motorcycle mechanic. The Weasel is *dead*…and I'm a hotshot motorcycle mechanic.

Pause.

Bartender: How do you like my head?

Healey: *Pumps his fist.* It's perfect!

FIFTEEN

Ken McCoo wears the uniform of a security guard. Enters and announces himself.

McCoo: I'm Ken McCoo and I'm home from the bloody wars! *Silence. He moves cautiously toward a bed in a darkened corner of the room.* Hiya, treasure. Are you napping? Do you want to come out for a while? Watch some TV…?

Helen: *Very weak.* No. I'm fine in here.

McCoo: It's stuffy in here. And dark. What do you say we open the curtains up, let some sunshine in, some air… *Opens the curtains.*

Helen: *No!*

McCoo: Helen *look*, it's a beautiful...

Helen: SHUT THEM!

McCoo: Okay okay... *He does. He sits on the edge of the bed.* Oh, Helen...we have to have a talk about this.

Helen: I wish I were dead.

McCoo: No you don't.

Helen: Yes I do.

McCoo: The operation was successful, honey. Everything went okay, there's nothing physically wrong with you anymore, Dr. Deerborn said...

Helen: THE DOCTOR ABANDONED ME!

McCoo: Helen...

Helen: *He saw something inside of me! He saw something inside of me and lo! It disgusted him and he runneth from the surgery and it broke up his marriage and it made him go into the desert!*

McCoo: Ssshhh. Ssshhh.

Helen: I'M EVIL AS HELL INSIDE!

McCoo: No you're not.

Helen: I'm filthy inside, my body is not my friend anymore —

McCoo: You just...

Helen: My body is against me!

McCoo: ...you just settle down. Do your deep breathing.

Helen: I'm tired of breathing.

McCoo: Do your deep ones.

Helen: I'm tired.

McCoo: I'll come back in a little while. You lie there and do your deep breathing and think good thoughts about yourself and I'll make us some dinner.

Helen: My body isn't hungry.

McCoo: It will be.

Helen: Do we have any ice cream?

McCoo: That's my girl.

Helen: Close the door!

McCoo: I will. *Leaves bed.* Jesus loving God…

Lights up on **Kenny** *eating Cheerios straight from the box.*

McCoo: I didn't know you were home.

Kenny: I just got here.

McCoo: *Opens fridge.* What've you been doing all day?

Kenny: Boring myself to death.

McCoo: When does track-and-field start up?

Kenny: I'm not gonna do it this year.

McCoo: Why not?

Kenny: Because I'm not as good as Howie was.

McCoo: Sure you are. Will you help me with dinner tonight?

Kenny: I'm going out.

McCoo: You said you just got here.

Kenny: I just dropped in.

McCoo: Once in a while it'd be nice for you to have dinner with us, son.

Kenny: Sure, Dad. Me and you and the macaroni. Why don't we invite Alice over once in awhile?

McCoo: Because she wouldn't come anyway.

Kenny: That's because we never *invite* her.

McCoo: Don't we have any ice cream?

Kenny: I ate it.

McCoo: *Closes fridge.* Why don't you go in there and see her,

Kenny, she's your mother. She gave you birth and she gave you your love for animals and she —

Kenny: She's looney tunes, Dad.

McCoo: Don't get smart.

Kenny: I have to go. *Walks away.*

McCoo: *Follows him.* Where do you always have to *go* to, Kenny? You're only fifteen years old, you need to be at home sometimes. Come back here! *Kenny runs.* Yeh, sure, you little brat! Eat all the ice cream then run for the hills!

Silence. Somebody help me.

SIXTEEN

Howie: *Wearing space-age goggles and riding an exercise bike. His cell phone rings.* Hello?

McCoo: Hi, Howie. It's Dad.

Howie: Hi, Dad.

McCoo: Why're you breathing so hard?

Howie: Because I'm going uphill.

McCoo: You're what?

Howie: I'm riding my new exercise bike, Dad. It's amazing. It's linked to a virtual reality system that simulates different terrain and degrees of difficulty. Right now I'm biking across this stupendous tropical island. It's beautiful here, there's exotic birds and monkeys, little bridges and streams, a long gorgeous coastline and a bewildering assortment of women in tight and provocative jogging attire. There's one right in front of me with hipbones from heaven. How are *you* doing?

McCoo: Crummy.

Howie: How's Mom?

McCoo: We have to have a family meeting.

Howie: Oh. When do we have to have it? I'm pretty busy at the club these days.

McCoo: Soon. And I want Alice to be there too.

Howie: That could be difficult, Dad.

McCoo: Help me, sport.

SEVENTEEN

Phone rings and a message machine kicks in. **Alice McCoo** *is half-naked and snorting coke.*

Alice's voice: "Hi! This is the home of Alice and Brian and The Bull. *A dog woofs.* That's *pit*-bull. *The dog growls.* Nobody's here to take your call right now but it's very important to us that you leave your tedious message, let us stand here and scoff at it, erase it, and then go back to the time-consuming business of being snooty and reclusive. Here comes the beep: this better be good." *Beep.*

Howie: Alice, you're incorrigible. This is Howie. Dad wants us to meet him for drinks tomorrow and have, quote, *a family meeting*, unquote. Sounds like Mom-talk to me. I guess we'd better do it, huh? Give me a call back when you — *She picks it up.*

Alice: I don't want to, you go and represent both of us.

Howie: I shouldn't have to do this by myself.

Alice: This is what I have to say — send Mom to a big, white hospital on a little green island in the middle of the deep blue sea and let her make daisy chains for the rest of her natural life.

Howie: You're stoned again, aren't you.

Alice: Mr. Detective.

Howie: You have to come, Alice.

Alice: No.

Howie: Yes.

Alice: No!

EIGHTEEN

Trudy: Here's to our new and improved life together!

Healey: Here's to my clipped wings.

Trudy: Greaseball. *They clink glasses.* And here's to the guy who took a shot at the doctor who then dumped Tammy who then picked a fight with little ol' *me* who now has a *hunk* for a roommate! Isn't life strange how it all bumps along — b'doop b'doop — *Yes!*

Healey: This apartment feels weird.

Trudy: I know what! Let's go to The Brick tomorrow and buy something brand new to celebrate our start together. They have those desert patterns for sofas now that would go really good with my Indian rug and your cactus collection.

Healey: This ceiling feels low or something.

Trudy: What's eating you, Healey? Talk.

Healey: Trudy, I'm thirty-six years old and I've never lived with a woman before. I'm not too sure how good I'm going to be at this.

Trudy: Let's buy a new bed!

Healey: Is sex all you ever think about?

Trudy: Is that a wrench in your pocket or are you just glad to see me?

Healey: What's wrong with the old bed?

NINETEEN

IN THE DARK

Healey: ...No, don't...Szabo, c'mon, don't don't...

Trudy: Healey...?

Healey: No, Szabo, *no...*

Trudy: Baby…?

Healey: *NO!*

We hear a magpie yapping, which takes us into the next scene.

TWENTY

Trudy: Morning.

Healey: *Yawns.* Somebody go out there and shoot that bloody magpie.

Trudy: How'd you sleep last night?

Healey: Good. Great. Nothin' wrong with this bed.

Trudy: Who's Szabo?

Healey: What?

Trudy: Who is Szabo? You were talking in your sleep last night, you woke me up. You sounded very distressed. Talk to me, babe. No secrets. No secrets or it's trouble between us, I won't abide.

Healey: I haven't even had a coffee yet, Trudy, could ya lay off my ass just a little.

Trudy: I will not abide by secrets.

Healey: I have a hangover.

Trudy: Secrets will kill us.

Healey: Okay! *Pause.* Szabo's my father…was…he's dead now. He picked on me all the time. There I talked.

Trudy: Did he used to beat you up?

Healey: Yeh. He used to beat me up. Go make some coffee.

Trudy: Tell me everything, Healey.

Healey: That's everything.

Trudy: Don't ever forget I'm on your side.

Healey: Good! Get coffee!

Alice: Where's Kenny? How come Kenny's not here?

McCoo: *Glances at Howie.* Before you got here, Alice, I was telling this to Howie, that um...I haven't seen Kenny for a couple of days...and that it's another good reason for having this meeting this family is...

Alice: What do you mean you haven't seen him for a couple of days?

Howie: He took off.

Alice: Where is he, Dad?

McCoo: I don't know. He never tells me anything. All we ever do is fight and then he flies out the door.

Alice: Gee — sounds vaguely familiar.

Howie: Control yourself, Alice.

Alice: If you're gonna sit there and bitch at me all night...

McCoo: Kids...

Howie: Sorry, Dad.

Alice: Ouch!

McCoo: What's the matter, Alice?

Alice: Howie kicked me under the table!

McCoo: Howie...

Howie: Get on with it, Dad.

McCoo: Yeh. Um. As you know...Mom's been having some difficulty, after her surgery last month, getting her feet back on the ground. *Alice rolls her eyes.*

Howie: She needs more exercise. How is she eating?

McCoo: Not very well.

Howie: What does her doctor say?

McCoo: Her doctor...is, um...on some kind of leave of absence. He can't be reached for a while.

Howie: So go get another one then.

McCoo: Soon, next week. One of his underlings, Dr. Holiday, seems like a —

Alice: Oh come *on*! Mom needs serious professional help — *in the head!* Right? This is why we're gathered here — right?

Howie: Alice...

Alice: Well for Godsakes!

Howie: We're listening to you, Dad.

McCoo: Your mother... yes...she's very troubled. Confused about things. And I...um, I...don't know how to...what to... don't know where to... *He breaks down.*

Howie: *Sincerely.* Oh, Daddy...

Alice: There goes the reunion.

Howie: Shut your mouth!

Alice: That does it, I'm gone.

Howie: You're so gone it isn't even funny! Go look in the mirror, you've got some coke around your nose — I can *see* it, you little drug addict!

Alice: Watch it, sport — and you're vice-free.

Howie: I don't even *drink* anymore.

Alice: Word gets around, maître d'. Story goes you sleep with a different waitress every night. I'd say that falls in the realm of iniquity. Nay?

Howie: Well at least I don't *marry* them all to support my bad habits.

Alice: I hear this place is laundering money and you're taking whiffs off the rim to cover your gambling problem.

Howie: Four times, little sister, you've been married *four* times since you were seventeen.

Alice: How're the horses running?

Howie: You're only twenty-six!

Alice: Oh look, there's a vacant VLT!

Howie: Have you ever been on your own? Have you ever had a job?

Alice: Not with the mob!

Howie: Said the snow queen!

McCoo: Stop it! *Silence.* I came here to ask for your help. Well I don't want it. Don't need it. I'll take care of things myself. As usual. *Throws down a bill and leaves.*

Howie: Dad…?! *Pause.* We should both be shot and pitched into the same grave. He even bought the nachos.

Alice: *Shouts.* I want my little brother!

Howie: Alice… *Reaches for her.*

Alice: *Pushes him away.* Stop *Al*icing me!

Trudy approaches with a tray. She wears a referee's outfit that is barely there at all. She looks tired and depressed.

Trudy: Excuse me — you're wanted on the phone, Howie.

Howie: Who is it?

Trudy: I don't know.

Howie: *Rises.* What's the matter with you, Trudy, you look like shit these days. Go put some make-up on or something.

He leaves.

Trudy: *To Alice.* My boyfriend and I — we had another big fight last night…and this time I threw him out. And I think he might be dangerous.

Alice gives her a droll look.

Alice: Then go and get another one. They work in teams. One to beat you up and one to protect you. And then they switch. Go get me a drink.

TWENTY-FOUR

IN THE DARK

Wade: Well? Whaddya think so far?

Carol: It's…awesome, Wade. What is it?

Wade: What does it look like to you?

Lights up on Wade's sculpture.

Carol: It looks like…chaos.

Wade: Uh-huh. Sure. Calamity. The shambles. I'm calling it *Nervous Wreck.* And like I was saying, Carol, I've nearly run out of materials and that's a real drag because I'm going great guns on it right now and I don't have any more money to put into it and that big competition is coming up…

Carol: How much more do you need?

Wade: Well…including scrap metal, nuts and bolts, acetylene, paint, the rent on my studio, beer…um…couple of thousand? Two weeks, ten days, she's done.

Carol: She?

Both look up at Wade's weird metal sculpture again.

Wade: It? *She opens her purse.* What're you doing?

Carol: I'm going to write you cheque for two thousand dollars.

Wade: You're kidding. *She writes it out.*

Carol: Gift. My donation to the arts this year. The ballet, the theatre, the symphony…all of those great little jazz clubs back in the old days…Martin and I… *He reaches for the cheque.* …have always been patrons.

Wade: Gosh, Carol — *reaches for it again* — you don't know how much this means to me, I'm flabberghasted, I'm —

Carol: Take your shirt off.

Wade: *Peeling his shirt off.* You're a wonderful woman, Carol, you're my whole inspiration, before I met you I was floundering, I was —

Carol: Shut up. *She walks around him with the cheque.* Sebastion is coming home. He's flying in on Thursday. What're we going to say about ourselves?

Wade: Why do we have to say anything?

Carol: I don't think I can keep this a secret, Wade, it'll show right through. I think we have to come clean. Do you want to do it or should I?

Wade: I can keep it a secret.

Carol: Take off your jeans.

Wade: *Unbuckling, unzipping.* Carol...me and you...we're not exactly...pinning our whole *lives* together. We're just... having a truly great summer, right? And I mean...Sebastion is a pretty fragile guy and way more conservative than you might think and what with everything else that's happened...

Carol: Underwear. *He does.*

Wade: ...the drive-by shooting, your break-up...me and you... well it all might, um, you know, be just a little too...too much too... *He laughs. She stares him down.*

Carol: What the hell are you trying to say?

Wade: What do you wanna hear? *Pause.*

Carol: That very first night after we made love you said something to me, it's been stuck in my head ever since, you said that I screamed. I was drunk, I don't remember, I need some clarification. What do you mean I screamed?

Wade: You were having a good time, Carol.

Carol: No, listen, I'm serious, pay attention — did I scream any words?

Wade: *Coy.* Maybe.

Carol: What words?

Wade: Well — *fondles her* — you said, um, hammer me, torch me. Bend me and bolt me. And I said, whatever you want, baby, and you screamed...

Carol: What?

Wade: Hallelujah.

Carol: Liar.

Wade: Why is this so important?

Carol: Because I've been waking myself up at night screaming and my therapist thinks I'm trying to expel something from deep in me that's poisoning me and he thinks I picked *you* as a kind of conduit for drawing that, whatever it is, poison, out. You're a bright boy, what do you think?

Wade: *Beat. Laughs.* Man, I think you analyze things WAY too much. It's sex! Sex is *noisy* sometimes. Why don't we quit talking about it and go and lie down.

He reaches for her — she lets out a long scream. Then silence.

Wade: You want to know what you screamed that night? *He holds out his hand and she puts the cheque in it.* You screamed your husband's name.

Pause.

Carol: Make love to me one more time and don't leave anything out.

TWENTY-FIVE

Hooker: Want some company?

McCoo: What? *He's carrying a Safeway bag.*

Hooker: Are you looking for some company?

McCoo: *Beat.* Oh! Um. No, I was...I'm on my way home. I have to make some dinner...for the family.

Hooker: You look sort of lonely.

McCoo: Do I?

Hooker: Yeh.

McCoo: Well. Um. I work by myself most of the time, at night, on weekends. It can be sorta...whatstheword...

Hooker: Lonely.

McCoo: I guess I've never really thought about it that way before.

Hooker: Y'wanna go upstairs with me for a little while?

McCoo: What? No! I mean...thanks, but — but I don't think I could do that.

Hooker: Could or should?

McCoo: Both. Both.

Hooker: You've earned it, Ken McCoo. You deserve some treats in your life. You work damn hard just to keep things going and it's all uphill: sickly wife, dissolute offspring...even the family doctor has turned his back on you.

McCoo: Who are you? Do you know me from somewhere?

Hooker: Come here for a second. Just let me put my hand down your...

McCoo: I have to get going!

TWENTY-SIX

Helen: Who's there? Who is that? Ken, is that you?

Kenny: It's me, Mom.

Helen: Kenny?

Kenny: Yeh.

Helen: Are you home from school already?

Kenny: We're still in August, Mom.

Helen: Are we?

Kenny: Yeh.

Helen: Has track-and-field started up yet?

Kenny: I dunno. Mom...Mom, how come...how come you won't get up? Dad said the operation worked, he says you can get up anytime you want to now.

Helen: No. No, Kenny, your Dad...your Dad is a mighty fine

man but he doesn't really understand what's going on inside of me.

Kenny: What *is*, though?

Helen: You just worry about your own life, sweetie. There's mountains to climb and races to run and girls to meet...

Kenny: GET UP! *Silence.*

Helen: Kenny...listen...the thing is this. My body isn't exactly *me* anymore. We're having a kind of split from each other.

Kenny: What're you talking about?

Helen: Well, it's like what they always used to say in Sunday school: there's the Flesh and then there's the Soul. They live with each other for as long as they possibly can and when the relationship finally runs its course, for *whatever* reason, they parteth company. In my case now...the Flesh is full of Messages...and the Soul is tip-toeing away. To join the Beautiful Army. Let nature run its course.

Kenny: How did you *get* this way?

Helen: Well that's the million dollar question, isn't it. I think... well I *used* to think it was just the luck of the draw: some people get leukemia, I get The Thingy. But the more I think about it...the more I believe I was *chosen* for it.

Kenny: What do you mean?

Helen: I believe these Messages were *put* in my body for a purpose.

Kenny: What kind of purpose?

Helen: Don't tell Daddy. *Whispers.* To give Dr. Deerborn a clue from another dimension.

Kenny: What?

Helen: I was up on the ceiling in the operating room looking down at myself, I was having one of those out-of-the-body experiences, and the doctor was fiddling around inside of me and he saw some kind of instructions in my entrails and he had to get after it quick. That's why he ran away from the surgery, I'm not mad at him anymore, it *had* to have been important. He delivered you, Kenny. Need I say more? We are all bound up together in this like one big family. Dr. Deerborn has some kind of huge fight on his hands and he needs *all* the help he can get. Cancer rhymes with answer. Wink, wink.

Kenny: *Beat.* I have to go now, Mom.

Helen: Are you making dinner with Daddy tonight?

Kenny: No. I think I'm going out with some friends.

Helen: Are you going to a movie?

Kenny: *Shrugs.* I don't know.

Helen: Go to a nice one, sweetie. There's too much crap on shows these days. It'll rot your brain. And thanks for hopping by, Kenny-boy. No matter what happens you'll always be my little bunny-wabbit.

Kenny: Sure, Mom. *He starts to leave. Turns back.* Mom?

Helen: Yes, dear?

Kenny: If Alice calls...if Alice ever calls...would you tell her that I...I don't know, nevermind. Bye, Mom.

Helen: Smooth sailing.

TWENTY-SEVEN

Trudy: There've been times in the last little while when I needed you a lot but I didn't know how to find you. When they told me you'd up and quit your job I didn't know where to turn to. It was just lucky I saw you on the street today so I followed you, trying to get my courage up, trying to find the right words. *Beat.* Damnit, Tammy, please talk to me. *Pause.*

Tammy: I'm living with an East Indian prince in a castle in Upper Mount Royal.

Trudy: *Laughs.* Goofball.

Tammy: It's the truth.

Trudy: You're kidding.

Tammy: His family made zillions in computers and he's a regular playboy. This is the first weekend I've been in town since I met him. We travel everywhere. Last week we were in Egypt, the week before that, Brazil. We have a swimming pool. *Shows her ring.* And he wants me to marry him.

Trudy: Holy shit.

Tammy: He's nice to me, impossibly generous, intelligent, sexy, worldly...

Trudy: But...?

Tammy: He has other women. It's a cultural thing.

Trudy: Are you sure you can handle this?

Tammy: *Little snort.* You forget who you're talking to, kid.

Trudy: Right.

Tammy: And what have *you* been doing for excitement?

Trudy: Well mostly like before I guess...except that I'm living with Healey now.

Tammy: In our old apartment?

Trudy: Yeh. For now.

Tammy: And so how is it going with Healey?

Trudy: *Lies.* Good! Great! His work is going well and mine is going well. We're going camping on his bike for the long weekend. Up around Nelson, those hot springs. Do some hiking, some caving...

Tammy: It's good to have things to look forward to.

Trudy: Yeh. It is.

Tammy: Get *it* before it gets you: that's *my* motto.

Trudy: *Nods.* Yeh.

They don't have anything else to say to each other.

TWENTY-EIGHT

Sebastion: It's good to be home. You look great. So what's all this stuff you said we needed to talk about?

Pause.

Mom?

Another pause.

Hey! When did you start painting your toenails?

TWENTY-NINE

*Wade cuts off his acetylene torch and lifts up his face shield. The **cellist** is actually here in this scene, playing throughout.*

Wade: Sebastion.

Sebastion: Wade.

Wade: When did you get home?

Sebastion: Couple of hours ago.

Wade: How was Europe?

Sebastion: Groovy.

Wade: Did you paint lots of pictures?

Sebastion: A few. *Looks up at Wade's sculpture.* That's quite the piece of...workmanship *you* have going there.

Wade: Thanks.

Sebastion: I didn't say I liked it.

Wade: Don't you?

Sebastion: Is it supposed to be portentous of something... a tangle of things to come?

Wade: Yeh. Sort of.

They listen to the cellist for a moment.

Wade: She calls herself EuLaLa. She's a street musician. She's broke, she doesn't have anywhere to go, so I said she could hang out here until she gets her bearings.

Sebastion: She plays well.

Wade: Yeh.

Sebastion: Are you sleeping with her?

Wade: No. *Beat.* She doesn't ever go to bed. Honestly, I haven't seen her in bed yet, she either sleeps sitting up or doesn't sleep at all, I don't know. *Beat.*

Sebastion: My father, the country doctor, loves cello. He even owns one. Inherited it. Can't play it. Won't. Poor bastard: he's gone off his rocker you know. He took his gun and he's living in a hotel room down by the tracks. Before I came over here I looked for it...the gun I mean...and when I asked my mother where it was she burst into tears. My father, the country doctor, isn't worthy of her tears. Poor sad thing. *Beat.* How much have you taken her for...you pernicious whore?

Wade: She's a grown up woman, Sebastion.

Sebastion: She's under your spell.

Wade: *Little laugh.* Oh I wouldn't say that.

Sebastion: Wade, my mother is the only woman I've ever really loved and you're the only man. I'm so jealous and mad I could scream. I don't trust myself, I might do anything.

Wade: *Beat.* Did you tell her we were lovers?

Sebastion: Yes.

Wade: I bet that went over big. So what were you going to do with your father's gun if it *had* been there?

Sebastion: I don't know.

Wade: Shoot me?

Sebastion: Either you or Mom. Or both of you. Or my father. Or all of you. Or all of you and then myself. Or just myself.

Wade: That's a lot of bloodshed.

Sebastion: Yes.

Wade: So now what?

Sebastion: I don't know. Cry?

Wade: *Offers his hand.* Come up here. Don't be afraid. I'll show you what I'm doing.

THIRTY

Deerborn sits on the bed handcuffed to the bedpost. He looks terrible.
Hardball sits in a chair watching television. It's an action movie.
Explosions, gunfire, loud music.
Long pause.

Deerborn: How much is my wife paying you to keep an eye on me?

Hardball turns the TV down.

Hardball: What?

Deerborn: How much is my wife paying you to keep an eye on me?

Hardball: The starting rate. Two hundred and fifty dollars a day plus expenses. It goes up every ten days. *He turns the TV back up. Beat.*

Deerborn: What kind of expenses?

Hardball: *Turns it down again.* What?

Deerborn: What *kind* of expenses?

Hardball: Mileage, accommodation. In case you skip town, you know. She said to follow you.

Deerborn: How did you find me?

Hardball: Tricks of the trade. *He snaps a picture of Deerborn.*

Deerborn: Did she find you in the Yellow Pages or something?

Hardball: No, I sort of found her. In a bar. She was alone. Looking downsy-wownsy. You know, so I asked if I could buy her a drink, normal thing. And she said no. So I bought her one anyway and we started to talk. She was wearing a purple dress cut way down the back between her shoulder blades. You know that one?

Deerborn: Yes.

Hardball: She said you had a gun.

Deerborn: It's in a safe place.

Hardball: Where? *Pause.* I don't know what happened between you two but it can't be worth killing yourself over. What was it? An infidelity?

Deerborn: Yes.

Hardball: Why?

Deerborn: I don't know. That's what I've been doing up here. I've been trying to give it a name.

Hardball: Pussy.

Deerborn: I don't think it's that simple.

Hardball: Your wife, she must've been a real knockout once. Don't get me wrong, she's pretty nice now — but twenty years ago, eh? Eh? Good in bed? Nice ass? Come like a choo-choo?

Deerborn: Do you enjoy your work, Hardball?

Hardball: Lookit, Doc — I'll tell you something about me — I don't give a flying fart about your miserable marriage or your screwed up life. *Takes a picture of him.* I'm in it for the money. *Takes another picture.* Guys like you give birth to guys like me.

Deerborn: Two hundred and fifty dollars a day. How often do you work?

Hardball: Not often enough. It's a lousy job. I used to play in a rock band. Should've stuck with it. *Pause.*

Deerborn: I was a real beatnik back in the early sixties. Those were great days, Hardball. That's when I met my wife. I'm sitting in a smoky basement café with a bottle of red wine in one arm and Carol in the other. Everybody's singing, we're drunk and we're happy, we're full of passion and nonsense and possibilities. Everyone we know is falling in love or living in Paris or making low-budget movies. We couldn't think of anything worse than becoming lukewarm members of society. Clang goes the trolley, spits electric, and the jazz rolls round and round. *Beat.* We went home together that night. We read Leonard Cohen in bed. We got married in Mexico.

Pause.

I'll give you a thousand dollars if you take the cuffs off and get out of here, Hardball. That's four days' work. I mean how long do you think you can stand it up here with me?

Hardball: What're you talking about, we're just getting to know each other. We live fascinating lives, me and you. I got shot at once. You want hear about it?

Deerborn: *Two* thousand. Cash. It's in my pocket.

Hardball: If you kill yourself I'll feel bad.

Deerborn: *Five* thousand. We'll go to a bank machine.

Hardball: Your wife is screwing someone. I went and watched them once. I even took some pictures, you want to see them? Hell, if I were you I'd go and kill *her.*

Deerborn: You bastard! Who are you?! *He jerks on the cuffs violently.*

Hardball: Rattle your cage, Dr. Deerborn. Rattle your miserable cage.

Deerborn: What do you WANT? Name it!

Hardball: I want your miserable soul.

Deerborn: You got it.

THIRTY-ONE

Trudy is on the phone at the sportsbar.

Trudy: Hi, Howie. This is Trudy. Um. I'm phoning from the club. I just found out from Sue you were cutting my hours in half. Um. Look I'm...I mean I know I've been kind of messed up lately but I really need this job and I'll make it

all up to you, the way I've been acting. Um. So I was thinking, since I'm free tonight, and if you were going to be at
home…that maybe I'd drop over there and apologize to you
in person…anda…see what happens. Okay?

THIRTY-TWO

Kenny McCoo is at a pay phone outside a pool hall.

Kenny: Hello is Alice there? Do you know when she might get
back? This is her brother. What do you mean? Oh. Where
is she then? If you did anything bad to her I'll come over
there and kill you. *He hangs up.*

A moment — looking lost — then he picks up the phone again.

THIRTY-THREE

*Deerborn sits staring at the TV that is turned down. He has a gun in
his hand. The cuffs are gone and so is Hardball. A long moment like
this then he puts the gun in his mouth. Another long moment. There's
a knock at the door. He takes the gun from his mouth and stares at it.
Another knock. He panics and throws the gun out the window, then
immediately regrets it.*

Deerborn: Damn!

*Another knock. He goes to the door and swings it open to reveal
Ken McCoo.*

McCoo: Hello, Dr. Deerborn.

Deerborn: You think you're a real hero now, don't you.

McCoo: I beg your pardon?

Deerborn: Do I know you?

McCoo: Ken McCoo. Um. You operated on my wife a little
while ago. Helen. Um. You took something out. A growth
of some kind.

Pause. They stare at each other.

Could I come in for a few minutes and talk to you, Doctor...about my wife? She isn't doing very well and I could really use some advice.

Deerborn: Are you some kind of lawman or soldier or something?

McCoo: Oh! *Looks down at his uniform, laughs.* Well kind of. I'm a security guard for Caterpillar Incorporated, I just came from work. Twenty-five years last fall. They gave me a real nice pocket watch. Look I'm really sorry for bothering you like this, Doctor. I phoned your house. Um. Your wife...she told me where you were, she...seemed to think it would be okay if I came up to see you...here.

Deerborn: Who did you say you were?

McCoo: Ken McCoo. *He takes out his pocket watch and opens it to the inscription.*

Deerborn steps aside. McCoo enters.

Deerborn: What do you want?

McCoo: Dr. Deerborn...my wife, Helen, who you operated on... is kind of mixed up about things. Um. She seems to think... that...her whole body...because she had to have surgery on it...has...somehow turned against her. She says it's dirty, gone bad. Her mind has...well...I'm afraid...I'm really afraid she's trying to hurt herself over this...this trauma... of... having to have surgery...and it keeps getting worse and worse every day, I...

Deerborn: Metastasis.

McCoo: Metas...

Deerborn: Metastasis.

McCoo: *Swallows hard.* What's that?

Deerborn: It's the transfer of a health-impairing agency to a new site in the system, a secondary growth, a...conveyance of some...bad thing. Like a real cold draft in the house moving from room to room.

McCoo: Is it treatable? Can you break it?

Deerborn: I can barely even say it.

McCoo: Jeez!

Deerborn: Things are pretty scary, aren't they.

McCoo: *Sits on the bed.* My whole darn *family* scares me. This thing with my wife is really tearing us apart. Mind you... we've...sort of *always* been...prone to disturbances. I mean just like you said...like a draft, like a conveyor belt... *dominoes....* Once something bad starts to happen in our family it just seems to want to keep rolling.

Deerborn: *Nods.* Yes. *Pause.*

McCoo: Anyway...this *metasta*-thing you were talking about... I guess we'll just have to wait for a while and see where it takes us, eh? And maybe, God willing, it'll go right *through* my house and run its course elsewhere and in the process make us stronger. That's something to hope for. Right, Doc? Isn't it? *Beat.*

Deerborn: Sure thing, Mr. Caterpillar. You and your whole darn family are going to be just fine.

McCoo: *Sighs deeply.* Thank you.

A train goes by outside. The whole room shakes like crazy. A picture falls off the wall. Then the train fades away.

McCoo: Well! *Smacks his knees and stands up.* I guess I'd better be going now and let you get back to what you were doing. *Walks to door.* I can't thank you enough for taking the time to talk to me, Doc. It's meant a lot to me. *Opens door....*um. But if you don't mind me asking you, Doctor...? What... what kind of leave of absence are you on? I mean, what're you actually...*doing* up in here?

Deerborn: *Beat.* I'm learning to play the cello. *McCoo glances around the room.* In my head.

McCoo: Oh. Well. Good luck at it, Doc.

McCoo exits. Deerborn remembers the gun and goes to the window. He looks around but can't see it.

THIRTY-FOUR

Howie: I'm sorry for every fight we've ever had and I'm sorry for being such a lousy brother and I'm sorry your marriage didn't work out again. You're my sister and I love you, you can stay here for as long as you want to and I'll help you however I can. We'll look out for each other, sis, we'll be our *own* family, just me and you and to hell with the rest. Okay?

Alice: *Laughs.* Well there's a teeny bit more to it than even that.... Brother dearest.

Howie: What do you mean?

Alice: I'm pregnant.

Howie: Oh.

Alice: I've been careless — 'bout everything.

Howie: So does whathisname Brian know?

Alice: No.

Howie: Is it his?

Alice: Maybe.

Howie: Are you going to keep it?

Alice: I don't know yet. Does it WANT to be kept?

Howie: Maybe you'd be a good mother.

Alice: Yeh. Motherhood. Glorious frigging motherhood. *Cries out.* I HATE MYSELF!

Howie holds her as she sobs.

Howie: No you don't, no you don't.

His intercom buzzes.

Who the hell...?

He goes to his security box and pushes a button.

Howie: Yes?

Trudy's voice: It's Trudy. *Howie smacks his forehead.*

Howie: Just a second, Trudy. *To Alice.* She works at the club — we've had a little falling out...

Alice: I'll walk around the block. How long does this usually take?

Howie: I'll tell her to go away, you're more important than any of my...

Alice: In-between snacks?

Howie: Alice...

Alice: Who am I to cramp your style. I'll grab a hotel some-where. Not to worry.

Trudy's voice: Howie?

Howie: *Into intercom.* Just a second! *Back to Alice.* Are you sure?

Alice: *Getting her coat.* Look, Howie, the reason I came over here wasn't to crash on your sofa or even to get your sympathy. The break-up was coming, I'm not in a panic about it. I came over to see if you wanted to go and look for Kenny with me. I found out he's been sleeping in an all-night pool hall way up in Little Italy somewhere.

Howie: This family drives me crazy. I'll go with you tomorrow.

Alice: I can't wait for tomorrow. That's okay.

Howie: You should learn to drive, Alice.

Alice: I've always had boyfriends.

Howie: Do you want me to call you a cab?

Alice: That's okay, I'll flag one.

Howie: If you find him...tell him...tell him from me not to quit track-and-field. I love you, sis. If you ever need to talk about anything...

Alice: *Kisses him.* Yeh yeh. *She goes to the door.*

Howie: Are you really going to be okay?

Alice: Life rambles on.

She opens the door to reveal Trudy standing there looking a bit sheepish.

Trudy: A guy came out of the building so I...

Howie: Hi Trudy.

Trudy: *To Alice.* We're having a little trouble at work so I...

Alice: Bye Trudy. *She exits. Howie stands away from the door and Trudy enters slowly.*

THIRTY-FIVE

Healey: Trudy...?! I know you're in there, Trudy. Please, Trudy...please open the door and let me back in.... *Lis*ten to me, babe.... I'm talking to you — like a man — who really *knows* he has problems. I don't *want* to though...! Trudy...? I *promise* I won't ever strike you again. We have to start things over again — *please*, Trudy! You *promised* to be on my side! *Please!* THOSE ANTELOPES HAVE GONE BESERK AND THEY'RE RUNNING ALL OVER THE PLACE!

THIRTY-SIX

Carol and Sebastion are driving quickly through the city in a police car that flashes its lights and sounds its siren as it goes through an intersection. Long pause.

Sebastion: You hate me, don't you.

Carol: No, Sebastion, I don't hate you. I don't have any space *left* to hate you, I'm consumed with hating myself.

Sebastion: Well I hate Dad — and so should you.

Carol: *Glances at him. Shakes her head.* What the hell happened to us? I'm a terrible homemaker, that's what. You grew up soft and selfish and petulant and malevolent and it's all my fault.

Sebastion: I'm also a lousy artist, don't forget that.

Carol: I *pushed* you into the arts trying to fill up a hole in myself. And what I did with Wade was out of fear and rancor for my lost youth, my stale marriage, and *yes*, some revenge.

And *no*, your father is not a choirboy. But the man's human too. He's fifty-five years old and he's troubled about his life — his vocation, his sexuality, mortality — and he's full of ghosts which go way back into his childhood and he's tormented by things less speakable and knowable...like we *all* are.

Sebastion: He wishes I'd never been born.

Carol: Oh Sebastion...

Sebastion: If it hadn't been for you getting banged up with me he'd probably be a concert cellist by now. Not a doctor. Which he loathes, pretends he doesn't, and takes it out on me.

Carol: *Looks at him.* That's an odd bit of math.

Sebastion: You think I'm clueless but I'm not.

Carol: We would've gotten married anyway, Sebastion. We loved each other deeply. You were a bonus — honest. Don't you believe that?

Pause.

Sebastion: When I was just a little boy — you won't remember this — we were living in that blueish-green apartment. I was lying in my bed. You were doing something in the kitchen and he was out in the living room by himself, he was studying for some exam. He closed a book, he walked across the room, he rubbed the bow across his cello and it startled me, made me cry, it sounded like a monster — and you yelled at him to stop it. And ever since then he's resented me.

Pause. Sebastion sulks. Carol puts her hand in his hair.

Carol: No, Sebastion, I *don't* remember that. But wonder of wonders — the tangled up web of us.

He cuddles close to her.

Sebastion: Oh Mom. *Beat.* Me and you, and Wade.... I mean we're nearing a brand-new millennium, right? Where survivors explore new territory and survivors hunger for new truths and survivors invent new rules.... I mean, I mean Mom, Mom I believe you knew, on *some* level, when you took Wade as your lover...well...I honestly be*lieve*, that you knew, un*conscious*ly maybe, that he and I...

Carol: Get your hand off my breast, Sebastion.

Sebastion: *Suddenly.* Look! There he is! *Hoots.* My father, the country doctor, thinks he's Spiderman!

THIRTY-SEVEN

Deerborn is standing on a ledge beside a window high above the hotel parking lot. We can hear pigeons and distant traffic. There's a man in uniform and sunglasses leaning out the window trying to talk to him.

Thorpe: Dr. Deerborn? Dr. Deerborn, I'm Staff Sergeant Horatio Thorpe. You took a bullet out of me once and I've always been very grateful for that. Let's have a little chin wag you and me, us two old warriors from the same planet earth. Would that be okay, Dr. Deerborn? Your wife and your son are on their way, they are very concerned for your total well-being and they told me to tell you you *have* their loving support. Talk to me, Doctor. Say something. *Beat.*

Deerborn:

> Give me back my house
> Give me back my young wife
> I shouted to the sunflower in my path
> Give me back my scalpel
> Give me back my mountain view
> I said to the seeds along my path
> Give me back my name
> Give me back my childhood list
> I whispered to the dust when the path
> gave out
> Now sing
> Now sing
> sang my master as I waited in the raw wind

Beat.

Leonard Cohen.

Thorpe: Can't say I recognize it.

A police car pulls into the parking lot below them with its lights flashing. Thorpe looks down.

Thorpe: *Speaks into two-way.* Thorpe. Yeh. Bring them right up here...quick.... This guy's doing birdy calls. Out.

He looks at Deerborn again.

> Hang in there, Doc, we'll get this thing figured out. You're a valuable member of society, buster, don't go anywhere. *He ducks back inside the hotel room.*

Deerborn:
> I whispered to the dust when the path gave out
> Now sing now sing

THIRTY-EIGHT

*The city moves round and past **Shep**'s car like a fluid of light and colour and contour to give the sense of motion, surreal motion. They are passing a mickey of vodka between them.*

Tiger: Show it to him.

Kenny: You guys are driving me crazy.

Tiger: Show him it.

Shep: Should I?

Kenny: There isn't anything, you're just teasing me.

Shep: Should I show it to him?

Tiger: Show it.

Kenny: Jeez you guys...

Tiger: Show him, Shep.

Shep: I don't know. He might freak out.

Tiger: No he won't.

Kenny: Why would I freak out? What is it? Show me. Liars.

Shep: Should I?

Tiger: He says to.

Shep: Should I show him it.

Tiger: He's *dying* for it.

Shep: Well if he's absolutely *dying* for it I guess I better then. I sure wouldn't want anybody *dying* if they didn't have to.

Tiger: Show it!

Shep: Don't freak out.

Kenny: Why would I freak out?

Shep: Just don't. I'm being serious now.

Shep reaches between his legs beneath the seat and brings out a gun.

Kenny: *Gawks at it.* Holy shit.

Tiger: Told you. *Giggles.*

Kenny: Where the hell did you get that?

Shep: I found it.

Kenny: Is it loaded?

Tiger: Yes!

Kenny: Where did you *find* it?

Tiger: Tell him. This is so crazy, Kenny. Tell him!

Shep: At The Sandman hotel. I got this weird little guy to go into the liquor store there for me and I was just waiting for him to come back out again and I saw this black thing lying there in the middle of the parking lot. Ten feet away. And it looked like a gun. So I got out and went over to it. And there it was and it *was* a gun.

Tiger: Somebody must have thrown it away after killing somebody, that's what I think.

Kenny: And it's loaded?

Shep: *Cracks it open.* Those are bullets, Kenny.

Tiger: Let him hold it.

Kenny: I don't want to hold it.

Tiger: I did.

Shep: Let's go shoot it off somewhere.

Tiger: Let's go!

THIRTY-NINE

Thorpe: How're you doing, Doc? Do you need anything? I'm a team player.

Deerborn:
>Have I come so far for this
>I wondered as I waited in the pure cold
>ready at last to argue for my silence
>Tell me master
>do my lips move
>or where does it come from
>this soft total chant that drives my soul
>like a spear of salt into the rock

Thorpe: Don't look down.

Deerborn:
>Give me back my house
>Give me back my young wife

He begins playing "air cello" — hard and passionately, as if for his very life.

FORTY

HIGH UP ON A HILL

Shep: What's there to shoot at? I can't even see anything from up here. Whose idea was this?

Tiger: Just shoot it.

Shep: I want to hit something.

Tiger: Shoot a tree.

Shep: What's that over there?

Tiger: Where?

Shep: Over there.

Tiger: I don't know where you're looking.

Kenny: Garbage can.

Shep: That's too easy.

Kenny: You couldn't even *see* it a second ago.

Shep: I thought it was something else.

Kenny: Have you ever even *shot* a gun before?

Shep: Yes, my Dad's.

Kenny: Liar.

Shep: You're starting to get on my nerves, Kenny.

Tiger: Shoot it!

Shep: I will!

He aims — and fires. Tiger jumps up and down with glee. Kenny rubs his ears.

Shep: Let's go somewhere else.

FORTY-ONE

Alice: What's going on?

Jogger: *In a red track suit.* I dunno, I was just jogging by, there's somebody on that ledge up there.

Alice: Wow.

Jogger: Other people's lives, eh?

Alice: Yeh. No kidding. *Looks around.* I thought The Sandman was supposed to be a *nice* place. This is a dump.

Jogger: You've got the wrong one — there's a newer one down on the strip.

Alice: *Sighs deeply.* I don't even know my own city anymore. I live in rooms. Cab drivers take advantage of me. I haven't had a suntan for years. I've got to get *out* more.

Jogger: *Looks at her.* Would you like to go have a beer somewhere?

She looks at him. Then laughs.

Is that a funny question?

Alice: Sort of. I mean I've been saying yes to that particular one since I was sixteen. I'm starting to think it's something about me that needs to be fixed. Or at least toned down.

Jogger: Tone it down tomorrow.

Alice: *Reconsiders, then:* Thanks but no thanks.

Jogger: No harm in trying, huh?

Alice: No harm.

Jogger: Maybe we'll meet again sometime. Under different circumstances. *They both look up.*

Alice: Right. Really romantic. *He jogs off.*

FORTY-TWO

Carol leans out the window.

Carol: *Carefully.* Martin? *Beat.* Martin, it's Carol. Everything is going to be all right now. Please come home. *Beat.* I never stopped loving you, Marty. Let's go home and pick up the pieces. Yes or no?

Pause.

Deerborn:

Come my darlings
The movies are true
I am the lost sweet singer whose death in the fog your new
high-heeled boots
Have ground into cigarette butts

Carol: From our first night together.

Deerborn:

You restless bullets
Lost in swarms
From undecided wars:
Fasten on
These nude throats
That need some decoration

Carol:

> And you over there
> My little acrobat:
> Swing fast
> After me
> There is no care
> And the air
> Is heavily armed…

Together:

> And has
> the wildest aim.

Long pause.

Carol: I know how tortured you must be.

Deerborn: I can see our neighborhood from here.

Carol: Come home, Marty.

Deerborn: I've been feeling my soul, like an oyster, moving around in its shell. There must be some kind of delicate hinge in there that connects the soft parts of my being to the bony parts, I mean it's a very…un*easy* feeling. Have you ever had that feeling, Carol?

Carol: *Nods.* Most of my adult life, my love.

A moment, then she climbs out onto the ledge with him. She takes his hand and they gaze across the city together.

Carol: This city's getting so big.

FORTY-THREE

Trudy: What's going on up there, mister?

McCoo: I dunno, there's two people on that ledge, I was just walking by…on my way home.

Trudy starts to cry.

McCoo: Are you okay?

Trudy: Yeh. No. *He holds her in his arms.*

McCoo: I know. Sometimes nothing ever seems to go right…boy do I know.

Dr. Doc Holiday walks by. He's very drunk.

Dr. Doc Holiday: *Sings.* Oh give me a home, where the buffalo roam, and the deer and the antelope…

FORTY-FOUR

IN THE CAR

Shep: Let's make up a game.

Tiger: Okay.

Shep: We all pick a colour. Then we drive around until we see a colour which *is* one of those colours and the person who picked it has to shoot at it.

Tiger: No matter what it is?

Shep: Yeh. It's like Russian roulette but different.

Long pause.

Tiger: Blue.

Shep: Green.

They both look at Kenny.

Shep: Pick one, Kenny.

Tiger: He'll pick one.

Shep: He doesn't have to pick one if he doesn't want to though. Don't let anybody push you around, Kenny, you have your own mind.

Tiger: He'll pick one.

Kenny: I have my own mind, Tiger.

Shep: You may have your own mind, Kenny, but it's *my* car and *my* gas and *my* game. And those three things put together are very much bigger than your mind is. So. If you don't pick a colour in about thirty seconds I'm going to drive you home to your wacko house and you will never be invited out with us again.

Tiger: *Kennnyyy...*

Kenny: Don't push me!

Shep: ...twenty-eight, twenty-nine, thirty.

Kenny: Let me see it first, Shep...just let me hold it first.

Shep: *Smiles.* Sure, Kenny. I understand.

He hands the gun to Tiger who hands it to Kenny who hesitates, then takes it. He holds it in both hands, not like a gun.

Shep: Like something warm and alive...right? Right, Kenny?

Kenny: Heavier though...heavier than what I thought it'd be.

Shep: Hold it how you're supposed to.

Kenny holds the gun properly.

That's it. That's right. That's what it really feels like. And there's nothing else in the whole wide world that feels quite like it. Ex*act*ly like a gun. The perfect thing for your hand. It actually snuggles back. Can you feel that, Kenny? Can you feel it snuggling back?

Kenny: *Nods.* Yeh.

Tiger: Way ta go, Kenny. *She starts rubbing his inner thigh.* Pick a colour. Pick a colour now, Kenny.

Kenny: Okay.

Tiger: Say one then.

Kenny: Um. Red.

Tiger: That's what I was going to pick and then at the very last moment I changed my mind.

Shep: So did I.

Tiger: Isn't that weird.

Shep: Okay. Here we go. We're looking for red.

We can hear Kenny's heart pounding...

FORTY-FIVE

…and pounding, getting louder and louder, as the lights rivering around the car become ecstatic. He's holding the gun in two hands, looking, looking.

We see the jogger in red from Scene forty-one stretching out his muscles beside the road.

Kenny's heart is pounding wildly now…

Kenny: My Dad never gave me a nickname.

And the cellist plays.

END

DRUMHELLER OR DANGEROUS TIMES

A CAUTIONARY TALE IN TWO ACTS

129

Curt McInstry as John Gallagher. (Thomas Usher)

DRUMHELLER OR DANGEROUS TIMES was first performed by Prime Stock
Theatre in Red Deer from March 16 – April 1, 2001, under the direction
of Thomas Usher with the following cast:

John Gallagher: Curt McInstry

Hannah Bruce: Suzanne McDowell

Frank/Dr. Bloomfield: David Leyshon

Nicky: Lindsey Hodgson

Bobby: Jesse Bourne

Old Woman: Dodi McDowell

PRODUCTION

Set designer: Walter Foster

Lighting designer: Marcus Sirman

Costume designer: Jade Bokyung Kim

Sound design: Dave Clarke

Set construction: Gary Murray

Technical Director/Venue Foreman: Kirk Blake

A radio version of the story, THE CARBON MURDERS, was produced by CKUA in
1990. A screenplay version of DRUMHELLER OR DANGEROUS TIMES was awarded
the 2004 Writers Guild of Canada Jim Burt Screenwriting Prize and the Alberta
TV and Film Institute Award for Feature-Length/Mow Screenwriting.

CHARACTERS

John Gallagher, 38

Hannah Bruce, 30

Dr. Bloomfield, 27*

Frank Bloomfield, 27*

Nicky (Mrs. Snow), 20

Bobby (Mr. Snow), 21

Old Woman

* Dr. Bloomfield and Frank Bloomfield can be played by the same actor

PLACE

Several locations in the badlands of southeast Alberta, minimally rendered,
suggesting the natural vastness of landscape and sky against the human
images of claustrophobia and entrapment.

TIME

1924 and the present

ONE

AMPHITHEATRE IN THE PRESENT

Young **Frank Bloomfield**, *with projector and remote, is addressing an audience.*

Frank Bloomfield: The badlands of southeastern Alberta are as mysterious and haunting as any place on earth. Here's some typical views of the landscape. It's like something from another planet. The first time I was here it blew me away. It still blows me away. Note the deep rills and complex system of pipes, the spooky hoodoos and dangerous cliffs. Imagine the heat, the cries of coyotes and nightowls. Trekking through a valley at dusk is an overwhelming experience. My grandfather was an early paleontologist, he came to Alberta from England in 1922. His journal, which I've only recently discovered, is equal parts data and poetry — he writes, "When the golden rays of the setting sun strike the stratograph of silt and sand and coal and clay in an antediluvian cliff wall above you the result can be breathtaking, ecstatic."

TWO

THE MOUTH OF GALLAGHER'S MINE, 1924

Gallagher *holds a lantern.*

Dr. Bloomfield: Are you sure it's safe in there?

Gallagher: I'm a coalminer, Doc. That's my bleeding livelihood in there.

Dr. Bloomfield: Has to be safe, 'course it does.

Gallagher: It's never fallen on me.

Dr. Bloomfield: Encouraging words. *Starts to go in.*

Gallagher: Yet.

Dr. Bloomfield: *Stops.* If it wasn't so blasted dark... *Gallagher laughs.* Don't confuse me with a sissy, Mr. Gallagher. In my calling I've scaled cliffs, endured sandstorms, trudged miles and miles in blazing heat. I just don't like enclosures, and especially dark ones. Is that a crime in this region?

Gallagher: Not that I'm aware of.

Dr. Bloomfield: Something from my childhood, I don't know...

Gallagher: Do you want to see my dinosaur or not?

Dr. Bloomfield: Lead the way.

They enter mineshaft.

THREE

OUTSIDE HANNAH'S BED-AND-BREAKFAST

*A young woman, **Nicky**, carries a ragged old teddy bear, and a young man, **Bobby**, a suitcase. They look completely spent. **Hannah Bruce** sees them coming and sizes them up.*

Bobby: Anybody here!

Hannah: Good morning. Are you looking for a bed?

Bobby: Our car broke down. We've been walking for an hour. It's hotter than blazes out here.

Hannah: Come on in then, get out of the heat.

Nicky: I need something to drink. *She collapses on the steps.*

Bobby: That's all we need is a medical problem.

Hannah: I'll get some water.

FOUR

INSIDE GALLAGHER'S MINE

Dr. Bloomfield: My God.

Gallagher: What do think of it then?

Dr. Bloomfield: It's marvelous.

Gallagher: Walked right by it for more than two years and one day it just glared out at me. Sneaky devil.

Dr. Bloomfield: Stupendous.

Gallagher: What is it?

Dr. Bloomfield: I need more light.

Gallagher: Here.

Dr. Bloomfield: God I've never — I don't know. Dromaesaurus? No, bigger. I need more light!

Gallagher: I'll rig some up for you later, Doc.

Dr. Bloomfield: My God, a new species?

Gallagher: Is it worth anything?

Dr. Bloomfield: Inestimable.

Fade to black. The sound of water being poured. In the dark, Bobby's voice:

Bobby: I got what the woman had, I got one egg and one beef.

FIVE

HANNAH'S GUEST ROOM

Nicky sits on the edge of the bed with her dress pulled up past her thighs and her feet in a tub of water. She sponges her legs. Her teddy bear and the suitcase rest on the bed.

Bobby: You take your pick, I don't care either way. Nice bath? You've been crazy for one for days. I can bathe in the river but I know you can't. *Unwraps sandwiches.* We're in a place called Carbon, it's a coalmining town and this whole area is known as the Drumheller Badlands. The woman who runs this house told me you can find fossils around here. She said all you have to do is walk in any direction into the hills and you'll likely see some. She said they're lying all over the ground. She also said they have rattlesnakes and scorpions. I read in a magazine once there are some creatures in the desert who don't have to urinate because of their sweat glands which are so robust —

Nicky: I don't need to know about urinating desert creatures.

Bobby: *Admires sandwiches.* She cut the sandwiches in half at the angle. I like sandwiches cut at angles. I don't know, it reminds me of something. Church picnics. Have one.

Nicky: It's too damned hot.

Bobby: You have to eat something.

Nicky: I drank some water.

Bobby: *Eats.* The woman who runs this house told me something we didn't quite count on, kid.

Nicky: And what is *that?*

Bobby: There ain't no road to Alaska. *She looks at him.* They've been talking about it since the gold rush but it ain't been built yet.

Nicky: I don't understand you.

Bobby: There ain't no road, it ain't been built.

Nicky: Then how do people get up to Alaska if *not* on a road? Flap their bloody wings?

Bobby: Well from here they usually go west to the city of Calgary and they get on a train and they go over the mountains to the city of Vancouver and then they get on a ship and they *float* to Alaska. The woman who runs this house told me a friend of hers took that trip once and she really liked it. She said they saw some whales on the way.

Nicky: I'm afraid of deep water, you *know* that.

Bobby: It's a big ship. It's like a big floating hotel. They have casinos aboard. *He does a drumbeat on the suitcase.*

Nicky: Just a second. You *told* the woman we're bound for Alaska?

Bobby: We need to know how to get there, don't we. *Another drumbeat.*

Nicky: I think we might've consulted a road map first.

Bobby: I told her we were on our honeymoon, from that place called Medicine Hat. And we're pure as the driven snow *Grins.*

Nicky: We should discuss these things before you go shooting off.

Bobby: The woman said her boyfriend knows about cars. When he comes by for his lunch she'll ask him to help us out.

Nicky: I'm so weary of the road I could weep, I'm so tired of sleeping in the car I could *scream.*

Bobby: They taste better. *She looks at him.* When they're cut at the angle. *Grins.* Taste better. *Chews.*

Nicky: *Picks up bear. Deep voice.* We think you've gone round the bend. *Bobby laughs.*

SIX

HANNAH'S PARLOUR

Gallagher: This is Dr. Bloomfield. He's come all the way from the university in Edmonton to look at my dinosaur. I told him your guest room was vacant.

Hannah: It's nice to meet you, Doctor.

Dr. Bloomfield: The pleasure's all mine.

Gallagher: Hannah Bruce.

Dr. Bloomfield: Miss Bruce. *They shake hands.*

Hannah: You really should've consulted me, John. This morning a young couple from Medicine Hat came to my door. Their car has broken down between here and Drumheller and they've temporarily taken my room. His wife collapsed on the step from heat exposure. They're on their way to Alaska for their honeymoon. I don't know what's wrong with their car but I promised you'd help them with it. *To Dr. Bloomfield.* John knows about cars.

Gallagher: I know one or two things.

Dr. Bloomfield: Well that's one or two more than I know. But listen, I'll go get a hotel room up the street, not to worry.

Gallagher: Hotel's closed down.

Hannah: This whole town is falling on bad times.

Dr. Bloomfield: Is the coal running out?

Gallagher: No, there's lots of coal. Problem is a big conglomerate out of Drumheller has all but absorbed the whole industry here and people are moving away. Town's dying.

Hannah: John is one of the last independent miners in the Kneehill Valley — and he's got his heels dug in.

Dr. Bloomfield: The man's political.

Gallagher: No, I'm just too old to learn any new tricks.

Dr. Bloomfield: I'll go get a room in Drumheller.

Hannah: John, why don't you go take a look at that broken down car first. Maybe it's not so serious and those two upstairs can be on their way after they've rested up a bit.

Gallagher: That's a good suggestion.

Hannah: I'll go fetch the man. They're both only kids really. Newlyweds. *She exits.*

Gallagher: Why would anyone want to go to Alaska on their honeymoon?

Dr. Bloomfield: Romance? The lure of the wilderness?

Gallagher: When I get back from looking at their car I'll rig some more lights in my mineshaft for you. What happens next?

Dr. Bloomfield: I'll do some scratching about, nothing major as yet, then I'll make some photographs and take them back to Edmonton for inspection and possible identification. But honestly, Mr. Gallagher, I don't think I've seen one like it before. This is very exciting.

Gallagher: You said it might be valued at something.

Dr. Bloomfield: A new find is always a — oh. Are you talking about money, Mr. Gallagher?

Gallagher: Is it worth any money?

Dr. Bloomfield: Not exactly, I mean…when this happens…when somebody finds a bone on their property…well, a few summers ago a rancher from outside of Steveville found a whole skeleton, a Corythosaurus —

Gallagher: I read about that in the paper.

Dr. Bloomfield: Yes — well — he donated it to the museum in Ottawa.

Gallagher: Donated.

Dr. Bloomfield: Mr. Gallagher, this is a very new field of science. There's scarcely any money to be had for research and diggings let alone for rewards.

Gallagher: Nothing for me then.

Dr. Bloomfield: Your name on a plate, in a book…

Gallagher: I thought we could sell it somewhere.

Dr. Bloomfield: I'm not a collector, Mr. Gallagher, I'm a paleontologist, those former days have all but gone. Has someone given you the impression that… *Hannah returns.*

Hannah: He's coming right down. Their name is Snow.

Gallagher: Mr. and Mrs. Snow.

Hannah: Honeymooners.

Dr. Bloomfield: Bound for Alaska.

Bobby enters.

Bobby: Which one is the boyfriend? Let's get at it.

He follows Gallagher out. Pause.

Dr. Bloomfield: So, you run a bed-and-breakfast, Miss Bruce.

Hannah: Yes.

Dr. Bloomfield: Is it profitable?

Hannah: No.

Dr. Bloomfield: Perhaps it'll catch on. This whole region is extremely fascinating. It's beautiful really. Mysterious.

I would think the tourist trade might be something to earnestly invest in here. A nice bed-and-breakfast...

Hannah: I'm making the attempt.

Dr. Bloomfield: I saw your sign on the road at the turn-off.

Hannah: Oh, is it still there?

Dr. Bloomfield: You don't get out of town very often.

Hannah: Everything I need is right here.

Dr. Bloomfield: I love this country — the seeming endlessness of it.

Hannah: You're British...?

Dr. Bloomfield: I was born in Manchester. Studied in London. Anthropology. Didn't have the foggiest about paleontology until I met Sternberg. Charles Sternberg? Along with Barnum Brown, Joseph Tyrell, he's on the cutting edge of the science. The three of them, and Weston, they've all dug here in the badlands. Sternberg said he hopes to come back, *if* he can find a sponsorship. Since the war though our work has been trivialized, cheapened by death as it were, the science of killing machines *growing* in esteem — I'm boring you. I talk too much I know I do.

Hannah: No, it's interesting. I knew we had petrified bones around here but I didn't know we were so famous for it.

Dr. Bloomfield: The surface has barely been scratched, so to speak. *Laughs.*

Hannah: You seem so young to be a doctor. You must be very smart.

Dr. Bloomfield: Oh I know a lot about bones and very little about anything else. I couldn't fix a car if my life depended on it.

Hannah: What do you think of John's dinosaur?

Dr. Bloomfield: I'm very excited about it — I don't know what it is.

Hannah: He thinks it might be worth something.

Dr. Bloomfield: Alas, we've had that discussion. *Turns his pockets out.*

Hannah: John's going broke. The Peerless Mine Company of Drumheller is choking him out of business. He has to give in soon.

Dr. Bloomfield: Bloody shame. I love the self-reliant spirit in man.

Hannah: Would you like a sandwich?

Dr. Bloomfield: I'd crave one.

SEVEN

THE HONEYMOONERS' CAR ON THE ROAD

Bobby: *To Gallagher under the hood.* What does it look like?

Gallagher: Water pump, I think. At *least* that. Might be some heat damage. How far did you drive when the heat gauge soared?

Bobby: The heat gauge doesn't work.

Gallagher: *Wipes his hands on a rag.* If I were going to drive across the continent in the middle of summer with my new beaming bride I'd make sure all my gauges worked first.

Bobby: That's damn good advice. Can you fix it?

Gallagher: Do you have another water pump?

Bobby: No.

Gallagher: Then I can't fix it.

Bobby: So what do you suggest then?

Gallagher: All I can do is tow it into Drumheller for you and park it at the service garage. Leave a note on the windshield.

Bobby: A note? What do you mean?

Gallagher: It's Sunday today. Everything's closed. Guess you honeymooners don't keep track of the time.

Bobby: Meaning we're stuck here.

Gallagher: Welcome to Carbon. *Smiles.*

EIGHT

GUEST ROOM

Nicky's feet in the tub, her dress to her thighs, sponging her neck and chest. Hannah comes to the door and listens.

Nicky:

> I'm nobody! Who are you?
> Are you nobody, too?
> Then there's a pair of us — don't tell!
> They'd banish us, you know
> How dreary to be somebody!
> How public, like a frog
> To tell your name the livelong day
> To an admiring bog!

> *To bear.* I memorized that poem on a rainy day in June when I was sweet sixteen. *As bear.* You were *never* sweet sixteen. *Herself.* Ain't it the truth.

Hannah: *Knocks.* Hello this room.

Nicky: *Bear's deep voice.* Yes?

Hannah: *Cocks her head.* Just seeing if you were doing all right. When you collapsed on the step out there I got a bit worried.

Nicky: She's doing fine now.

Hannah: Oh. And who do I have the pleasure…?

Nicky: Her bear.

Hannah: Well do you need anything, Mr. Bear?

Nicky: No, thank you, we're quite fine.

Hannah: I'm sorry I don't have any hot running water in the house, though I'd be happy to heat some up on the stove for you.

Nicky: We're having a sponge-off, it's very refreshing, thank you.

Hannah: They haven't got back from taking a look at your broken down car yet but I expect they will shortly.

Nicky: We're doing fine in here.

Hannah: Did she drink lots of water?

Nicky: Yes, ma'am.

Hannah: She has to keep her content up on a day like today or she'll get fatigued you know.

Nicky: Her content is up.

Hannah: I'll leave you both alone now then.

Nicky: *Herself.* Wait a second…

Hannah: Is that Mrs. Snow?

Nicky: Yeh, you wouldn't happen to have a glass of beer or a shot of whiskey or anything would you? Or both?

Hannah: We've got prohibition, honey.

Nicky: Know any bootleggers?

Hannah: I might.

Nicky: *Straightens up.* Jesus then, you don't suppose…

Hannah: Tell you what. You drink some more water and eat all of your sandwich and have a little nap and when the men get back from looking at your car we'll talk about this again. How does that sound?

Nicky: We'll resume with our bath. *Kicks up the water.*

Hannah: You do that.

NINE

FRONT STEPS

Dr. Bloomfield: *Writing in his journal.* The creature looks somewhat like a Dromaeosaurus "the running lizard" except it is bigger and has a flatter crown. Its eyes are large like Dromaeosaurus and its claws are also sickle-like. *Thinks.* The Kneehill Valley is some distance from the ancient swamp and delta where most of the dinosaurs lived. This creature lived in the surrounding redwood forest and was certainly a predator. *Thinks.* I see no way of excavating the

skeleton without disturbing Gallagher's mineshaft. *Thinks.*
Miss Bruce, the woman who owns this bed-and-breakfast,
has lovely large eyes, good teeth, and a shapely figure.
Thinks. Old Sternberg once said that the passions of Man
is all foolishness to God. *Thinks.*

Lights up on Gallagher writing a note.

Gallagher: Dear Ned:

Dr. Bloomfield: I don't believe in God.

TEN

THE HONEYMOONERS' CAR AT GARAGE

Gallagher: *Writing.* I think this car needs a water pump. Also
check the gaskets and hoses, etcetera, for heat damage.
The folks who own this vehicle are stranded at Hannah's
bed-and-breakfast in Carbon. Let's go fishing sometime.
John Gallagher. P.S. You still owe me forty dollars from
that card game. I haven't shot my pistol for quite a while
but I haven't forgotten how to.

Bobby: Strong words.

Gallagher: Have a way of working.

Bobby: Only if you mean them, son.

Gallagher: I shot at Ned in the month of July ten years ago.

Bobby: Did you hit him?

Gallagher: Wasn't trying to.

Bobby: What for? Another bad debt?

Gallagher: I caught him robbing a service station in Trochu.
I was a Mountie then.

Bobby: A what?

Gallagher: A Royal Northwest Mounted Policeman?

Bobby: Ah.

Gallagher: He stopped short in his tracks and we've been polite to each other ever since. So what do you do in The Hat, Mr. Snow?

Bobby: Beg your pardon?

Gallagher: What do you do in Medicine Hat?

Bobby: Oh. Various and sundry. I'm in between right now. Why did you quit the police?

Gallagher: They sent me to the war. I came back a different man you might say.

Bobby: You were over there, huh?

Gallagher: I was.

Bobby: I heard it was pretty bad.

Gallagher: It wasn't a picnic. Why Alaska?

Bobby: Why not? *Grins.*

Gallagher: *Sticks the note under the wiper.* I've got some chores to do. Let's go back to Carbon now.

Bobby: I'm much obliged for your kindness, Mr. Gallagher.

Gallagher: Don't mention it, Mr. Snow.

Lights up briefly on Nicky, stripped to the waist, posing with a revolver in the bedroom mirror.

Nicky: Some of this is true and some of this isn't.

ELEVEN

PARLOUR

Gallagher: I can't fix it, Hannah. We towed it into Drumheller. Maybe they can tomorrow, though there might be some heat damage which could take longer.

Hannah: These things happen.

Gallagher: Sorry, Doctor.

Dr. Bloomfield: I'll go get a room in Drumheller.

Bobby: I don't feel good about this, us barging in unannounced...

Dr. Bloomfield: You're stranded, it's your honeymoon...

Hannah: I have a hammock. *They all look at her.* Sometimes, when it's very hot out, I hang it between those two big trees behind the house. To sleep in.

Dr. Bloomfield: What an idea.

Hannah: It's quite comfortable really, and the creek is nearby...

Dr. Bloomfield: I've slept under the stars on many occasions. I *love* the fresh air, the sound of moving water...

Hannah: Then you wouldn't like the hotel in Drumheller.

Dr. Bloomfield: Then it's settled.

Bobby: This house is *full* of kindness.

Dr. Bloomfield: Mr. Gallagher?

Gallagher: Let's go rig those lights.

Dr. Bloomfield: Lead the way. *They exit.*

Hannah: Why don't you take the news to your wife about your car and ask her from me if she needs anything.

Bobby: I'll do that. *Starts to go.*

Hannah: Mr. Snow?

Bobby: *Stops.* Yes, ma'am?

Hannah: I'm sorry, I know you're stranded and that your visit here is quite unintentional...

Bobby: Everyone has to make a living, ma'am. We'll pay the full price for the bed, it's a lucky harbour.

Hannah: Thank you.

Bobby: *And* the breakfast.

Hannah: *Smiles.* Of course. And feel free use of the house and the yard. There's a swing set up on the east. Does your wife like to swing?

Bobby: I reckon she does.

Hannah: Well if you need anything…

Bobby: We'll ask for it. *He exits. Hannah watches him go.*

TWELVE

THE MOUTH OF GALLAGHER'S MINE

The doctor cleans his eye-glasses.

Dr. Bloomfield: Before I go back in there, Mr. Gallagher, there's something we ought to discuss.

Gallagher: I suppose I can guess. If that rancher at Steveville donated *his* dinosaur to the museum in Ottawa then it follows that I should, too.

Dr. Bloomfield: That's part of the matter, yes.

Gallagher: What else then?

Dr. Bloomfield: Well, if the excavation of these remains becomes a reality — and certainly there are obstacles, money the main one — well then it follows that your mineshaft would be disturbed for a while.

Gallagher: What length of a while?

Dr. Bloomfield: Hard to say — depending on the number of volunteers who could be mustered…a month or two?

Gallagher: How disturbed?

Dr. Bloomfield: I don't know really, I've never dug a skeleton out of a mineshaft before. It's painstaking work under the best of circumstances. Of course we'd be as delicate as humanly possible…

Gallagher: And meanwhile the business of digging for coal stands still.

Dr. Bloomfield: Would that be possible? You have to tell me.

Gallagher: I've no other livelihood, Doc.

Dr. Bloomfield: Mr. Gallagher, I realize how sensitive this issue is but —

Gallagher: Let me guess. If I was having to sell off my mine
to the conglomerate out of Drumheller —

Dr. Bloomfield: I *love* the self-reliant spirit in —

Gallagher: ...eventually, anyway...

Dr. Bloomfield: You've read my mind.

Gallagher: It's fair thinking. The boys from Peerless could
afford to shut this mineshaft down for *any* length of time.
Disturb the mine? By Jesus, destroy the damn thing,
they've hundreds in the region. They'd give me a good
price for my property and maybe even hire me back on
for wages.

Dr. Bloomfield: These *are* hard times.

Gallagher: And they're *dangerous* times as well. There's something you ought to know.

Dr. Bloomfield: You have my attention, sir.

Gallagher: In 1921 I was tried for the murder of Mr. John
Coward who was a director in the Peerless conglomerate.
And I was convicted and sentenced to hang. I sat on
deathrow, Doc.

Dr. Bloomfield: Good Lord. *Puts his glasses back on.*

Gallagher: Then, at the midnight-hour, I was granted a retrial
based on police mishandling of evidence and I was subsequently acquitted. The boys from Peerless and their fancy
lawyers were obviously disappointed. They wanted me,
Doc, and they almost got me. I believe I was framed. The
year before that, you see, I'd been an organizer for the
mine operators in Drumheller where I used strong-arm
tactics to break up the formation of the Kneehill miners'
union. Well it's sort of a long story with several emotional
tributaries but the upshot was I switched my allegiance
to the union and I redirected my modest powers against
the conglomerate. John Coward and I had been friends
and though I betrayed him politically I believe he felt no
personal animosity toward me — one of many who didn't —
and I didn't he.

Dr. Bloomfield: *Amazed.* You sat on deathrow.

Gallagher: I believe there are men who *still* want me dead.

Dr. Bloomfield: I'm speechless.

Gallagher: Well one might construe from this story that I should swallow my pride and sell my mine, even to my aggressors, and get out of town to save my hide, as it were.

Dr. Bloomfield: But that isn't in your make-up.

Gallagher: I fought in the Great War — I don't back down easily.

Dr. Bloomfield: I can see that.

Gallagher: And I'm Irish.

Dr. Bloomfield: To boot.

Gallagher: I'm up to my neck in legal fees from my trial and the business of coalmining gets ever more treacherous, so if you could find some way to get me a few pennies out of this dinosaur deal...

Dr. Bloomfield: It isn't very likely, Mr. Gallagher, I have to be honest.

Gallagher: *Beat.* Some kind of new species, huh?

Dr. Bloomfield: Do you mind if I look again, make some photographs...?

Gallagher: Doc, as far I'm concerned you can *sleep* in there with it.

Dr. Bloomfield: Oh, it wouldn't be the first time.

THIRTEEN

GUEST ROOM

Nicky sits on the end of the bed meticulously folding the wax paper from their sandwiches. Bobby stands at the window looking out.

Nicky: I'm glad we broke down, I like it in here.

Bobby: The woman who runs this house would like us to pay the full price for our stay.

Nicky: Don't get any ideas.

Bobby: And then there's the bill for the car repairs, gasoline and oil, the passage by train and ship, food and beverages.... Good thing we're loaded, huh? *She doesn't look at him.* Right, baby?

Nicky: How long will it take to drive to Calgary?

Bobby: About three hours.

Nicky: That's three bloody hours too long. I want to stay right here for about a month. I won't go out of this room. Keep bringing me things.

Bobby: We have to stick to our plans, Mrs. Snow.

Nicky: I don't remember the plans. I don't remember anything that came before this room.

Bobby: The plans are what they always were — they mean that we don't get caught. If you can argue with that then go right ahead though I doubt you can.

Nicky: I want to be someone else.

Bobby: I've had days like that.

Nicky: I'm not talking about *days*. I need to *die* and be born again differently! *Crunches wax paper and throws it.*

Bobby: Let me hold you. *Goes to the bed.* Didn't you take a nap? Let me rock you bye-byes. *He puts his arms around her from behind.* When I was in prison I used to spend hours wishing I was someone else. I'd stare at the ceiling in my cell and make up new names for myself, new lifestyles. I'd say to myself that being a gangster had too many drawbacks and I'd imagine myself coming home on the bus from a hard day's work at the office and kissing my wife and ten kids and getting my golf clubs out of the closet...

Nicky: You've never golfed in your life.

Bobby: Ain't it the truth.

Nicky: I can't imagine you as a father either. It actually makes me shudder.

Bobby: Exactly. *Rocks her.* Because y'see, kid, my best dream in prison was the one we're having now. North to Alaska. Work the casinos. Meet the right people. Money clamours to money and the rest is all chance. Alaska: the brave new world.

Nicky: I can't see past these walls.

Bobby: Well that's why *I'm* in charge of things.

Nicky: You're not in charge, you just do all the shooting off.

Bobby: I got us *this* far didn't I.

Nicky: That's a complicated remark, *Mr.* Snow.

Bobby: They ain't gonna catch us.

Nicky: I could sleep for ten days. *She closes her eyes.*

Bobby: I'm going to buy a charcoal-grey suit with white pin-stripes and a pair of burgundy shoes with white spats. And a Panama hat. I'll be the best-dressed man in Alaska. I'll have a pair of white-handled derringers under my coat and you at my side in a blood-red dress. *He kisses her neck.*

Nicky: Wake me when we're there.

Bobby: We're there in my head already, kid.

Nicky falls asleep. Bobby goes back to the window and peeks through the curtains where he sees Gallagher and Hannah in the backyard unfurling a hammock.

Bobby: So satisfied with themselves... *He aims at them with his finger.*

Hannah: This was Madam Tango's hammock.

Bobby: ...these Canadians.

Gallagher: Everything you *have* was Madam Tango's. You came to her with nothing but your tattered soul and dirty knees as I recall.

Hannah: That's a fact. *They start to hang the hammock.*

Lindsey Hodgson as Nicky and Jesse Bourne as Bobby. (Thomas Usher)

Nicky suddenly sits up with a sharp gasp. For a moment she doesn't know where she is. Bobby looks at her. She gradually gets her bearings, then:

Nicky: Blood everywhere.

FOURTEEN

BACKYARD

Gallagher: Dr. Bloomfield says there'll likely be no recompense for my dinosaur find, he says there's probably nothing in it for me at all except some recognition.

Hannah: I know. He told me, too.

Gallagher: I've had enough recognition.

Hannah: I realize that.

Gallagher: Do you like him?

Hannah: Who, Dr. Bloomfield? What do you mean?

Gallagher: What do you think of him? How does he strike you?

Hannah: I've only just met him, John.

Gallagher: You like refinement in people, does he impress you?

Hannah: I know you're teasing me.

Gallagher: Do you think he's handsome?

Hannah: Oh stop it.

Gallagher: Well-groomed, well-bred…?

Hannah: He's passionate about his work.

Gallagher: You like passionate men.

Hannah: I do. *He grabs her.* John!

Gallagher: My mineshaft is presently occupied and the work has ceased. And it's Sunday besides.

Hannah: Let's go inside then.

Gallagher: Right here. *He reaches up her dress. She pushes his hand away.* Since when did you get so prudish?

Hannah: You wish.

Gallagher: Why would I wish that?

Hannah: It's in your nature. You wish to conquer. Like the first time over and over again, the thrill of the kill forever.

Gallagher: You have a perverse mind.

Hannah: I know you don't really love me, John.

Gallagher: Don't I?

Hannah: Then marry me.

Gallagher: Not this again.

Hannah: If you love me then marry me.

Gallagher: That's *your* arithmetic not mine.

Hannah: It's because of how we met, I know it is. For all of your world experiences you're really quite narrow-minded. I don't fit into any easy category for you anymore, I'm sort of this and sort of that, not one plain thing or the other.

Gallagher: You argue too much.

Hannah: You don't like hearing the truth.

Gallagher: And what is the truth?

Hannah: That you can't imagine spending the rest of your life with a woman who was once your —

Gallagher: You're *still* that woman who was once my — *She goes to slap his face — he grabs her wrist. Freeze. He releases her, walks a ways off. Gazes into the hills.*

Hannah: I helped you through some hard times, John.

Gallagher: I didn't mean it to come out like that.

Long pause.

Hannah: When it starts to cool off let's take everyone up to those old Indian stones and watch the sun go down. It'll be fun. Can we?

Gallagher: You take them, I don't want to.

Hannah: Let's go inside.

Gallagher: Bribery.

Hannah: To hell with you then. *She leaves. He sighs. And as the lights fade we can hear Dr. Bloomfield whistling.*

FIFTEEN

THE MOUTH OF GALLAGHER'S MINE

A camera sits on a tripod outside the mineshaft. Dr. Bloomfield is at work within.

Gallagher: Doctor? *As he inspects the camera.*

Dr. Bloomfield: Yes?

Gallagher: How's it goin' in there?

Dr. Bloomfield: Very well, Mr. Gallagher. The lights you rigged up have been extremely useful. I thank you again.

Gallagher: Don't mention it. *He looks through lens.*

Dr. Bloomfield: Are you wanting something from me, Mr. Gallagher?

Gallagher: Miss Bruce is.

Dr. Bloomfield: Oh?

Gallagher: She wanted me to ask you if you'd like to take a little hike this evening. After it cools off. Up to a mesa where some old Indian stones are located. To watch the sun go down.

Dr. Bloomfield: I'd like that very much. The three of us you mean.

Gallagher: She's asking the newlyweds to come along, too. It's a great view of the badlands from up there. Romantic.

Dr. Bloomfield: Excellent. *Pause.* Are you still there, Mr. Gallagher?

Gallagher: I'm here.

Dr. Bloomfield: This bone of yours is embedded in the rock directly below the layer of coal. It's typical really. After coal-strata the number of dinosaur remains drastically drops off. The ancient forest here created the coal, you understand. It stands to reason then that the dinosaurs of this region departed, and quite suddenly actually, while the forests were still standing. It's a mystery really. I lean toward some kind natural catastrophe myself — famine, disease, a diabolical storm... *Beat.* Mr. Gallagher? Are you still there, Mr. Gallagher? *Gallagher says nothing.* Strange man.

Gallagher smiles and leaves.
A light wind rises up and streams into the next scene.

SIXTEEN

A VISION QUEST SITE OVERLOOKING THE BADLANDS

The wind swells, then thins into silence. Nobody speaks for a long moment.

Bobby: Lordy, what a view.

Hannah: I haven't been up here for ages.

Dr. Bloomfield: This formation of stones is a vision quest site. To the ancient aboriginals of this region it was a symbol of religious and communal stability. The sites were generally located at the highest point possible. Water had to be to the north or the south and the site had to have a clear, unobstructed view of the horizon in order to see the sunrise and sunset. When a young brave reached a certain age he would come to this spot with nothing but a piece of leather to sit on and a blanket for sleeping under, no food, no water, and the boy would stay here for some days until he saw a vision.

Nicky: *Standing apart.* What sort of vision? *All look at her.*

Dr. Bloomfield: I don't know really. Something personal, I expect. An omen, a sign, a message of some kind, the ghost of an ancestor...

Hannah: Wouldn't it be like having a powerful daydream? You know, like seeing yourself in the future... *Glances at Gallagher who remains looking at Nicky.*

Bobby: No food, no water? *Laughs.* Maybe something to *smoke* on?

Dr. Bloomfield: There's another stone formation not far from here called "Effigy Man". It actually looks like a man, much larger than this one. Nobody knows very much about it but all of the vision quest sites in the region clearly point toward it.

Hannah: Sun's going down.

Bobby: *To Nicky.* Where're you going, darling?

Nicky: *Departing.* I want to go for a stroll, do you mind, darling?

Bobby: Not a smidgen. I'm going to lie down for a little while and have a vision of myself in the future. *Quick thought.* Watch out for rattlesnakes! *He lays his head on a stone and his hat on his face….*and a Panama hat. *Laughs.*

Hannah moves closer to Gallagher who is gazing after Nicky.

Hannah: What do you find so interesting in her, John? Besides being young and pretty I mean.

Gallagher: I don't know yet.

Hannah: Well God, don't let *me* stand in your way. Go find out.

And with that she approaches Dr. Bloomfield who is writing in his journal. Gallagher glances over his shoulder at her and then, indeed, follows Nicky.

Hannah: You know more about our homeland than we do, Doctor.

Dr. Bloomfield: I studied anthropology, I read about these sites in a paper written by a fellow for the International Geological Congress. I have a near photographic memory — it's in my family, I don't boast. And no, Miss Bruce — *Closes journal* — I know *nothing* of your homeland. The notion of home is deeply personal.

Hannah: I like the way you talk.

Dr. Bloomfield: Please shut me up. This landscape! It makes me feel loony.

Hannah: It definitely has its way.

Dr. Bloomfield: *Looks at her.* Tell me about you. Who are you, were you born around here…?

Hannah: I was born in Calgary, I don't know who to, I was left on the steps of a church and raised in an orphanage.

Dr. Bloomfield: How did you find your way out here?

Hannah: It'll bore you.

Dr. Bloomfield: I promise it won't.

Hannah: I'd run away from the orphanage, I was living on the street. I met a girl who knew a girl who knew a coalminer who knew a bootlegger who knew another girl…

Dr. Bloomfield: I'm captivated.

Hannah: I became a Kneehill Valley prostitute.

Dr. Bloomfield: Ah.

Hannah: Saved me from starving I figure. And believe it or not I actually learned some self-respect. Madam Tango took me under her wing, I was special to her for some reason, so when she had that car accident coming back from Drumheller one night…well…she left me the house on her deathbed.

Dr. Bloomfield: The bed-and-breakfast you mean?

Hannah: I switched occupations.

Dr. Bloomfield: Apparently.

Hannah: The only thing I regret is putting the other three girls out of work. Or do I? Mixed feelings.

Dr. Bloomfield: Forgive me but…your house…it has *how* many bedrooms?

Hannah: Mine and the guest room, two. I see what you're thinking. Well it worked like this. The house was the gathering place where the coalminers came to, where the drinks were, the music, the girls. But we all had separate tents along the Kneehill Creek.

Dr. Bloomfield: You lived in a tent.

Hannah: Except in the winter — then we went lavish — got rooms at the Carbon Hotel. Still love the smell of canvas though.

Dr. Bloomfield: So do I actually.

Hannah: Especially when it's wet.

Dr. Bloomfield: Oh yes. *A moment, then he laughs.* Madam *Tango*?

Hannah: That's what she called herself, nobody knew her real name. She said she was from Buenos Aires, Argentina. She had some kind of accent, I don't know, I can be fooled. She had a box full of tango records though and she taught us all how to dance to it. Well she *tried* to.

Dr. Bloomfield: I'll wager you succeeded at it.

Hannah: In my own mind's eye.

Dr. Bloomfield: I would've liked to have been there — to have watched you.

Hannah: Madam once said that some music is meant to heal the soul but tango is here to keep the wounds open so you won't forget. *Beat.* Look at that sun. The horizon looks on fire.

Dr. Bloomfield: *Looks.* It really does. *Then he looks back at her.*

SEVENTEEN

SOME DISTANCE IN THE OTHER DIRECTION

Gallagher: Don't get too close to the edge of the cliff — it crumbles really easily. Isn't stable.

Nicky: Thank you. *She backs away.*

Gallagher: Why Alaska, Mrs. Snow?

Nicky: *Shrugs.* I don't know, it was *his* idea, he read an article in a magazine about it. I guess for adventure. We might change our minds though. How far are the mountains from here? I've heard about Banff, of course.

Gallagher: Part of a day's drive.

Nicky: Everything's so bloody far.

Gallagher: A part of a day isn't very long.

Nicky: Is for me. *Any* part is.

Gallagher: What do you do in The Hat?

Nicky: Beg your pardon?

Gallagher: What do you do in Medicine Hat? Have a job?

Nicky: I work in a bakery.

Gallagher: Is that where you met your husband? By the cin-
namon buns?

Nicky: It's none of your business where I met my husband.
She says politely.

Gallagher: He met no offense.

Nicky: I hear you found a dinosaur bone.

Gallagher: That's right. On the wall in the shaft of my coalmine.
Walked right by it for more than two years and one day it
just glared out at me.

Nicky: How old is it?

Gallagher: Dr. Bloomfield says it's *millions* of years. No one can
really know though. Or why they all died off.

Nicky: Not yet. People are too goddamned smart, they'll know
everything there *is* to know soon enough, it's just a matter
of time, there'll be no more secrets one day.

Gallagher: Now there's a sobering thought.

Nicky: My husband said you used to be a policeman.

Gallagher: For a while I was.

Nicky: You're Irish, right?

Gallagher: That's right.

Nicky: Raised over there?

Gallagher: Yes.

Nicky: How did you end up here?

Gallagher: Well I'd followed in my father's footsteps, you see, worked in the mines when I was young, got tired of it and joined the Royal Field Artillery as a gunner when I was only nineteen years old. Seven years later I was transferred to the Imperial Army Reserve and moved to Canada to be enlisted in the Royal North West Mounted Police at Calgary, then Trochu. And then I was sent to the war in Europe.

Nicky: Glad you got back.

Gallagher: I agree.

Nicky: To the glory of coal dust?

Gallagher: Not directly. First I joined the Alberta Provincial Police, spent two years with them.

Nicky: Why did you quit?

Gallagher: I was released.

Nicky: Why?

Gallagher: I was caught fraternizing with bootleggers.

Nicky: Speaking of which... *Suddenly we hear a rattlesnake...* that sounds close.

Gallagher: They're more afraid of you than you are of them. Just back away. *Suddenly a nightowl screeches — she gasps.*

Nicky: I want to go back to the house. *A coyote howls. She hurries away, stumbles...*

Gallagher: Watch your step!

Coyote howls again.
The loud rap of a mallet and Gallagher steps forward into a different light.

Gallagher: I didn't kill John Coward, Your Worship, and I don't know who did. I counted John as a friend. I was in the Great War and learned the value of friendship the hard way. The young man closest to me over there died in my arms and he'd saved my life only hours before. I

wept goddamnit. I balled like a baby. I'd never been afraid
of anything on earth before that tour of duty and now
I'm afraid of thunder and lightning which I used to love.

Anyway, the very next day, I get popped in the head by a
sniper's bullet. Goes right through my helmet. Next thing
I know I'm on horseback riding through sagebrush on the
side of a hill overlooking the Red Deer River. I'm wearing
a uniform I don't recognize and all I know is that my
horse is named Spirit. I think I've died and crossed over, of
course. Then I hear the cry of a coyote nearby and I follow
it to a patch of crocus where I find the poor beast caught
in a trap. Its leg is terribly mangled. It's mad with pain and
lunges and snaps at me.

Well, there's nothing left to do — I take out my service
revolver and I shoot it. And just then everything goes black
and when I open my eyes again I'm lying in a hospital bed
in London, England. My whole head is bandaged up like an
Indian turban. The nurse tells me I've been in a coma for
three and a half weeks. I don't remember my dream about
the coyote but I distinctly smell crocus.

Now if that isn't strange enough, Your Worship, when I
come home from that fucking bloodbath I join up with the
newly formed Alberta Provincial Police. You can see what's
coming. One day I'm riding my horse named Spirit on the
side of a hill overlooking the Red Deer River and I hear a
coyote crying which is caught in a trap. I have the strongest
sense that I've been here before and when I shoot the beast
I flash back to the battlefield and I live through my good
friend's death again.

Now the story's been offered here as evidence against
me that every so often without warning I lapse into a
kind of spell which can last for several minutes and when
I come out of it I often have some memory loss. It's
because of that wound to my head in the war. But what
I've not told anybody until this very moment is when
that spell happens I have hallucinations sometimes of the
things to come. I once had a vision of myself sitting right

here in this dock, Your Worship, and I'm sure you think that's funny but I know you're going to sentence me to swing today.

Now you're probably wondering what I'm getting at. Well I'm getting at this, that though I may be damaged goods in some respects and though I may be rough at times and though I may have killed in the war — I'm not a murderer. I feel like a coyote caught in a trap. So if you're so certain I killed John Coward then I beg you to take me out behind the courthouse and do away with me promptly for I can think of nothing worse than sitting on deathrow with only my innocence for company. That would be worse than the war to me. And that's all I have to say. Thanks for your indulgence.

EIGHTEEN

Nicky: *Shakes him.* Wake up!

Bobby: *Startled.* What's the matter?

Nicky: I want to go back to our room!

Bobby: I must've napped, it's nearly dark.

Nicky: C'mon, get up!

Bobby: Jesus, you're hands are trembling.

Hannah: *Approaching with Dr. Bloomfield.* Sun's down, I guess we better get going. It can be dangerous in the dark around here.

Dr. Bloomfield: We'll have the stars in a minute or two. It's a clear sky.

Bobby: *Wrenches his neck.* A stone for a pillow, that's a first.

Nicky: *Clutches his jacket.* Stand on your feet!

Bobby: Don't grab at me!

Hannah: Where's Mr. Gallagher?

Nicky: I left him over there by the edge of the cliff.

Hannah: *Calls.* John? *No answer.* Are you there, John? *Still no answer. Louder.* John?

Dr. Bloomfield: You sound concerned.

Hannah: He has seizures. From the war, a head wound. It can come without warning.

Dr. Bloomfield: Dear God — spread out — Mr. Gallagher?!

Hannah: John?!

Bobby: *Looks.* There he is.

Gallagher: *Strolls into view.* What's all the fuss about then? Somebody fall in a crevice?

Hannah: Just wondering where you were is all.

Gallagher: Daydreamin' is all.

Dr. Bloomfield: Well then, we're all together. The Carbon Hiking Party!

Bobby: *To Nicky, touches her face.* You've lost your colour, baby.

Nicky: *Pushes his hand away.* I need a drink.

Gallagher: Hold still, Mr. Snow.

Bobby: Why?

Gallagher: I'm deadly serious, lad. Don't move a muscle. Hold your breath. *He flicks something off Bobby's shirt collar.*

Bobby: What was it?

Gallagher: Scorpion. They sit under rocks in the heat of the day. Get lively at dusk. They're much smaller than most folks think, you know. *He holds his thumb and finger out to show just how small.*

Nicky: How do you people *live* around here?

NINETEEN

AMPHITHEATRE IN THE PRESENT

Frank Bloomfield: *With projector as before.* I hope you can see this, they're not very clear. These are a series of photographs taken by my grandfather in the summer of 1924. This is

the mouth of John Gallagher's coalmine along the Kneehill
Creek near Carbon which is only a few kilometres from
Drumheller. These next are of the dinosaur bone found
by Gallagher in the wall of his mineshaft. From these
photographs one can't be very sure what it was, though it was
likely Stenonychosaurus, a larger relative of Dromaeosaurus.
Note the large eye-sockets and the sickle-like claws. This
reptile was very smart and athletic. As a predator of this
forest it likely had no match. Here's a photograph of the
mouth of Gallagher's mine after it collapsed that summer.
The mine wasn't cleared until just *this* summer, after my
grandfather's journal was found, and with *my* persistence.
The dinosaur was entirely destroyed. But that's not the
end of the story. The excavators *did* find some bones in
the mineshaft — they were human bones.

*Lights up on the black mouth of Gallagher's mineshaft. The lights
burn brightly...*
Slow fade to black. Tango music.

[INTERMISSION]

TWENTY

THE VISION QUEST SITE IN THE PRESENT

*An **Old Woman** with a cane and a wide-brimmed hat stands gazing
out at the badlands. Frank Bloomfield approaches her. He has a knapsack
on his back.*

Frank Bloomfield: Hannah Bruce?

Old Woman: Mr. Bloomfield, I presume.

Frank Bloomfield: Call me Frank. *She glances at him.* It took me
    a long time to find you, Miss Bruce.

Old Woman: I wasn't hiding.

Frank Bloomfield: Why did you want to meet here? *She continues
    gazing out at the landscape.* Miss Bruce...?

Old Woman: *Glances at him.* You look a bit like your grandfather.

Frank Bloomfield: Do I really?

Old Woman: As I recall.

Frank Bloomfield: In what way? Please tell me. The few pictures I have of him are all so poor.

Old Woman: *Without looking.* Something around the nose I think.

Frank Bloomfield: *Absently touches his nose.* I have my grandfather's journal here, your name is mentioned in it several times. *He takes it out of his knapsack.* His last entry reads: "I don't know what to make of John Gallagher exactly. He's certainly a strange one, full of contradictions. He's rough but he's also insightful. His idea of establishing a dinosaur museum in this locale is quite enticing really. And Miss Bruce...a most intriguing woman. Capable, sensitive, sharp-witted, nice-legged..." And that's it — stopped in the middle of sentence.

Old Woman: He was a difficult man to stop in the middle of a sentence...as I recall.

Frank Bloomfield: I've heard that about him.

Old Woman: You never knew him?

Frank Bloomfield: No.

Old Woman: And what did you say you do exactly?

Frank Bloomfield: I work at the Tyrell Museum. Publicity, outreach, community engagement...

Old Woman: And how did you come by the journal?

Frank Bloomfield: Ah, it was found in the attic of an old house being torn down in Carbon. Your old bed-and-breakfast.

Old Woman: Really.

Frank Bloomfield: It was twisted up in an old hammock.

Old Woman: Ah.

Frank Bloomfield: Miss Bruce, I know your memory probably isn't quite what it used to be —

Old Woman: My memory is fine, Mr. Bloomfield.

Frank Bloomfield: What happened that summer my grandfather was a guest at your house? What do you remember?

Old Woman: I remember the heat.

Frank Bloomfield: Tell me about John Gallagher. I'll tell you what I know, I know that John Gallagher was a very good friend of yours and I know he was strapped for cash in the summer of '24. He had legal fees hanging over his head from his murder trial, his mine operation was going broke —

Old Woman: The conglomerate from Drumheller was choking him out of business.

Frank Bloomfield: I stand corrected.

Old Woman: What else do you know?

Frank Bloomfield: I know he was convicted of arson and was sentenced to ten years in prison for setting fire to the buildings on his property. At the trial he argued that someone had been hired by the conglomerate to do the deed but it didn't stand up. The judge determined he was attempting to collect the insurance, same judge who sentenced him to hang for killing John Coward. He went to prison and a few days later escaped. And he disappeared, never to be heard from again.

Old Woman: No, never to be heard from again.

Frank Bloomfield: Miss Bruce, we found some human remains in John Gallagher's mineshaft this summer.

Old Woman: Did you.

He removes a skull from his knapsack and holds it up so she can see it clearly, turning it around in his hands. The skull has a classification tag attached to it.

Frank Bloomfield: You see that, Miss Bruce? That little hole there? That's a bullet hole. *She peers closely into the face of the skull, in through its very eye-sockets.* The explosion which ruined the mine thoroughly scattered the body, too. *He tosses the skull from hand to the other.*

Old Woman: What exactly are you looking for, Mr. Bloomfield?

Frank Bloomfield: The truth, I suppose. You see I'd like to write a book about the region, about my grandfather partly, about the way things were back then...

Old Woman: Oh, you're very ambitious. *Laughs.*

Frank Bloomfield: Who was in Gallagher's mineshaft when it blew up, Miss Bruce? Do you know?

Old Woman: What if I did? Why should I tell you?

Frank Bloomfield: Because you want to? *Pause.*

Old Woman: I tire very easily, Mr. Bloomfield, I need to sit down now.

Frank Bloomfield: Give me your arm.

He helps her to sit. He offers her water from his canteen. She refuses, takes a flask from her purse and drinks from that instead. Then she gazes out over the landscape again.

Old Woman: This is a vision quest site.

Frank Bloomfield: Yeh I know. I've guided tours here lots of times. It points toward Effigy Man.

Old Woman: They all do.

Frank Bloomfield: Yes.

Old Woman: Does anyone know why yet?

Frank Bloomfield: No.

Old Woman: *She gazes out for a moment longer, then:* I was standing outside of the bed-and-breakfast that morning.

Frank Bloomfield: You have my rapt attention.

Old Woman: It was a very hot day.

Frank Bloomfield: Go on. *He sits beside her.*

Old Woman: *As the lights slowly narrow on her.* I looked down the road and I saw a young couple approaching on foot. They had a suitcase. She held a teddy bear. He said their car had broken down. She collapsed on the steps.

Tango music faintly, out of the past...

TWENTY-ONE

HANNAH'S PARLOUR

Tango music louder. Everyone has liquor. Nicky, drinking straight from a bottle, is clearly the drunkest.

Nicky: Thank God for bootleggers! *Drinks.*

Bobby: Go easy on that stuff—you know your own tolerance.

Nicky: Look after your*self*, Mr. Snowflake. *Wipes her mouth with a flourish.* I've never been happier!

Bobby: *To the others.* Her tolerance is kind of low.

Hannah: Did she eat anything?

Bobby: Not much.

Nicky: *Pressing against him.* Have you ever been happier, Doctor?

Dr. Bloomfield: Oh! Not recently, no. *Laughs nervously.*

Hannah: I could make some little crackers or something. Would she eat some cheese and crackers?

Bobby: I doubt that she would.

Nicky: Why are you talking about *her* as if she wasn't here?

Hannah: No offense, hon.

Nicky: She's *here*! She's here in this dismal little room and she's having a bloody good time of it!

Bobby: She'll pass out soon enough. She always does.

Nicky: This music makes her horny.

All stare at Nicky who poses.

Dr. Bloomfield: *Suddenly.* Teach me how to tango, Miss Bruce.

Hannah: I don't remember how to.

Dr. Bloomfield: It's like riding a bicycle, I expect. Throw caution to the wind! Come on!

Hannah: What the hell. *They begin to dance. With accent.* You 'uff to make your 'ole body rigid anda loose at the same-a-time.

Dr. Bloomfield: I'll be lucky to stay on my feet.

Nicky: I've never been a wallflower and I won't start now.
She grabs Bobby. Tango me, baby! Tango me up in knots!

Bobby: *Low to her.* Keep your dress on.

The four of them dance. A moment like this, then Gallagher slides out of the room unnoticed...except by Nicky.

TWENTY-TWO

GUEST ROOM

Tango music in background. Gallagher looks around their room. He finds a revolver in a jacket owned by Bobby. He finds their suitcase under the bed, opens it — and discovers a lot of money beneath some clothes.

Gallagher: American.

Now he hears footsteps. Puts it back under the bed. Nicky enters. She's perspiring from dancing.

Nicky: Looking for something?

Gallagher: You.

Nicky: Sniffed me out, tracked me down. *Moves into the room.* You could take advantage of me, Mr. Gallagher. I won't remember a thing tomorrow.

Gallagher: Is that the kind of man you think I am?

Nicky: You've been in a terrible war... *She starts to unbutton her dress* ....you've seen bloodshed...severed limbs...pandemonium...you're dangerous...you've been damaged...

Gallagher: And you're the blushing bride.

Nicky: Isn't it funny how some words... *As she lays down on the bed* ...sound exactly like the thing that they...you know what I mean...like splassshh. Like blussshh. *She laughs.* Do you know any words like that? *And with that she passes out.*

Gallagher: K'boom.

He bends over the bed and smells her hair and her throat. He touches her breasts. Then he exits.

TWENTY-THREE

PARLOUR

Bobby is passed out on the floor. Hannah and Bloomfield, laughing hard, dance to the end of the record. It's suddenly very quiet except for the phonograph needle.

Hannah: I can feel the ghost of Madam Tango in the house.

Dr. Bloomfield: Is she pleased with us?

Hannah: She thinks we're bloomin' idiots. *They both burst into a new round of laughter.* I think I sprained my ankle. *Limps to the phonograph player.*

Dr. Bloomfield: *Finds the bottle.* To the wounds of the day! *Drinks.*

Hannah: God my head is swirling.

Dr. Bloomfield: Who's the bootlegger in town?

Hannah: *Looks at him.* I am. *They laugh again.*

Dr. Bloomfield: You're a *most* intriguing woman, Miss Bruce.

Hannah: I'm just an orphan who ran away. The rest is all happenstance. Intrigue? No, I can't lay claim to any intrigue.

They gaze at each other. Gallagher re-enters.

Gallagher: *At Bobby.* The groom looks dead.

Dr. Bloomfield: 'Tis a powerful moonshine. Why *do* they call it moonshine? I wonder where that came from. Language! I'm forever fascinated…by it. *Laughs, sort of.*

Hannah: Where's the bride?

Gallagher: Same as he. *Nods upwards.*

Hannah: I better go look. Would you two men…? *She gestures toward Bobby.*

Dr. Bloomfield: Certainly. *Hannah exits. Beat.* Wonderful day!

Gallagher: Fascinating, yeh.

Dr. Bloomfield: The Carbon Hiking Party! *Laughs.*

Gallagher: Which end do you want?

Dr. Bloomfield: Lead the way. *They pick up Bobby and start to move him off.*

Gallagher: Why do they send them all to Ottawa, Doc?

Dr. Bloomfield: To Ottawa...?

Gallagher: Our dinosaur bones.

Dr. Bloomfield: Ah, well, because that's where the Geological Survey of Canada is located, the boys with the clout.

Gallagher: Why couldn't we have our *own* museum?

Dr. Bloomfield: That's a very good question, Mr. Gallagher. First you need a visionary...

Gallagher: That describes you.

Dr. Bloomfield: Willpower, stamina, money. Lots of all three, I'm afraid. The bones don't rise and stack by themselves. This lad has heavy feet.

Gallagher: Dances like it. *Lights up in the guest room.*

Nicky: Some of this is true...

Gallagher: And then there's the bride.

Hannah: Go back to sleep, honey.

Dr. Bloomfield: That one frightens me.

They exit with Bobby.

TWENTY-FOUR

GUEST ROOM

Hannah puts the covers over Nicky.

Nicky: ...and some of this...

Hannah: It's been long day for you.

Nicky: ...isn't...

Hannah: Go to sleep.

She puts the teddy bear in Nicky's arms. Gallagher and Bloomfield enter with Bobby.

Hannah: Thank you, gents.

They drop him on the bed beside his bride.

Gallagher: Two down, three to go.

Dr. Bloomfield: I shan't have another drop or I won't be able to work tomorrow.

Hannah: They look like children. *A moment...*

Dr. Bloomfield: Well! Think I'll call it a day then. Goodnight, you both. Thanks for everything.

Hannah: G'night, Doctor.

Gallagher: Don't strangle yourself in that hammock, Doc.

Dr. Bloomfield: *Laughs.* Tomorrow then. *He exits.*

Hannah: What were you two doing up here?

Gallagher: What do you mean?

Hannah: You disappeared together.

Gallagher: Not really.

Hannah: You left — she followed.

Gallagher: Hannah, listen, there's something —

Hannah: Aren't I enough for you anymore, John?

Gallagher: You're a fine one to talk.

Hannah: She's young enough to be your daughter *and* she's married *and* she's drunk!

Gallagher: Bloody hell yes and we had a quick go at it, too!

Hannah: Get out of my house! I hate you!

Gallagher: I know that you don't! Come here! *He advances on her and she strikes him several times on the chest.*

Hannah: You never wash your hands! They're always pitch black!

Gallagher: *Roars.* I'm a bleedin' coalminer! *Leaving.* Jesus, Mary
and Joseph… *Gone.*

*Hannah immediately regrets the incident and starts to go after
him — stops herself — looks down at the couple once more, sighs deeply,
then she exits too.*

*Another moment, then Bobby sits up and gazes at the door. Nicky says
something in her sleep. He looks down at her. Now she sits up as if in
a dream and the lights change.*

Nicky: They're fighting again!

Bobby: Are they?

Nicky: Can't you hear them?

Bobby: Sure I can.

Nicky: She acts so weird all the time, she belongs in a loony bin.

Bobby: Go tell me what they're arguing about?

Nicky: Okay.

*She gets out of bed and crawls across the floor to the door on her hands
and knees. Bobby laughs to himself as she goes.*

Nicky: *Her ear at the door.* It's about how he drinks too much.

Bobby: One of these times he's going to go for the gun.
He'll shoot *her* and then he'll come up here and shoot *us*,
I wouldn't put it past him.

Nicky: Don't say that!

Bobby: *Bear's voice.* Come back to bed, honey girl.

Nicky: It's freezing out here. *She hurries back into bed.*

Bobby: Let me hold you. *He does.* Did he touch you again?

Nicky: Not for a while.

Bobby: Where does he touch you? *Under the covers.* Here?

Nicky: Yes.

Bobby: Like this?

Nicky: Yes.

Bobby: *In her ear.* Let's capture some of those big moths with brown wings tomorrow.

Nicky: Okay.

Bobby: Close your eyes.

She does. Bobby claps his hands.

Nicky: There! He hit her! *She covers her ears.* Is it over? *He uncovers her ears.*

Bobby: Let's run away.

Nicky: Where to?

Bobby: Way up north somewhere.

Nicky: Can we take the puppies?

Bobby: We better, he's going to drown them, he said he was.

Nicky: No! *She hugs her teddy bear.*

Bobby: Back to sleep now.

Nicky: I don't know if I can.

Bobby: Would you like some of your cough syrup? That always helps.

Nicky: Okay. *He puts his hand to her mouth. She drinks from his hand and sinks back to sleep.*

Bobby: Sweet dreams, kid. *He kisses her.*

TWENTY-FIVE

BACKYARD IN THE MOONLIGHT

Dr. Bloomfield: *Writing in his journal.* "I don't know what to make of John Gallagher exactly. He's certainly a strange one, full of contradictions. He's rough but he's also insightful. His idea of establishing a dinosaur bone museum in this locale is quite enticing really. And Miss Bruce…a most intriguing woman. Capable, sensitive, sharp-witted, nice-legged…"

Hannah: *Approaches him.* Aren't you sleeping yet?

Dr. Bloomfield: Oh, Miss Bruce! No, I'm…just jotting down some notes.

Hannah: Can you see okay, I could bring you a —

Dr. Bloomfield: No, the moon is…I'm done now. *Closes journal.*

Hannah: I sort of unwound tonight.

Dr. Bloomfield: I as well.

Hannah: I don't like going to sleep when my head is swirling like this though. *He laughs.* Just some fresh air…before I turn in. *Beat.*

Dr. Bloomfield: Beautiful sky.

Hannah: A few clouds in the west though. Might be a thunderstorm coming. How's the hammock?

Dr. Bloomfield: Excellent! Thank you so much! Great idea!

Hannah: If it starts to rain come in and sleep on the chesterfield.

Dr. Bloomfield: Thank you, I'll do that. *Pause.* Are you all right? I couldn't help but hear…I'm sorry, it's none of my business.

Hannah: *She avoids the subject.* How long do you think you'll be staying?

Dr. Bloomfield: Just tomorrow, after lunch or so. Take some photographs of Mr. Gallagher's dinosaur, drive back to Edmonton…and then depending on Mr. Gallagher's decision to clear his property for excavation…

Hannah: He's in a difficult position.

Dr. Bloomfield: Yes.

Hannah: And he's Irish.

Dr. Bloomfield: Oh yes.

Hannah: Are you married?

Dr. Bloomfield: No.

Hannah: Girlfriend?

Dr. Bloomfield: Miss Bruce, I think you're the most incredible woman I've ever met — Oh God! — I've had too much to drink — please forgive me!

Hannah: I think you're very charming.

Dr. Bloomfield: No, I'm sorry, my big mouth. Your mouth. Your eyes in the moonlight...

Hannah: I love him.

Dr. Bloomfield: *Rises.* I'll leave immediately, I'll get a room in Drumheller...

Hannah: Sit. *He does. She sits beside him.* Doctor, I think we can convince John together to sell his mine to Peerless. In his heart of hearts I believe he knows it's the only thing to do. But he's tempting fate, you see. If he doesn't leave the region then one of these days someone will try to kill him and he thinks he's invincible.

Dr. Bloomfield: He told me his story, the war with the miners' union, his time on deathrow...

Hannah: He's lead a rough life.

Dr. Bloomfield: I can barely even imagine it.

Hannah: I wouldn't want you to be intimidated by him though. What I mean is, I wouldn't want you to abandon your ambitions without a good fight.

Dr. Bloomfield: I'd fight to the death I think. I might become famous, you know.

Hannah: I can see that in you, I really can.

Dr. Bloomfield: Miss Bruce...if Mr. Gallagher *could* be convinced to give up his mine...and he *did* leave the region...I assume you'd go with him?

Hannah: *Gazes into the sky.* John was the first man I ever had sex with and he was the first one I ever made love to as well, different occasions, of course, and I've worked very hard since then to try to *normalize* our relationship and I've come to believe if I could just get him *away* from here...

Dr. Bloomfield: But you also love this land.

Hannah: I've dreamed of raising children here.

Dr. Bloomfield: *Turns away.* I see your quandary.

Hannah: *Goes to him now.* Doctor, is there anything you'd like to do which you've *never* done before and to *hell* with the consequences?

Dr. Bloomfield: At the moment you mean?

Hannah: Ever. If you had one choice. *She drags off his hat.*

Dr. Bloomfield: *Thinks.* I'd like to go to China.

Hannah: Why?

Dr. Bloomfield: Dig for bones. *Shrugs.*

Hannah: *Smiles.* I think I'll let you sleep now. *She returns his hat to his head then leaves. He peeks into the sky...*

Lights up on Nicky standing beside the creek with her teddy bear.

Gallagher: *Walking nearby, sees her.* What're you doing out here by the creek, Mrs. Snow? You're a ways from the house.

Dr. Bloomfield: Anybody up there?

TWENTY-SIX

THE CREEK NEAR GALLAGHER'S MINE

Nicky: *Childlike.* Woke up. Needed some air. And you?

Gallagher: I live over there, that's my shack.

Nicky: I saw you pull up in your car.

Gallagher: My dog's run off, I've been looking for him. Seen a dog?

Nicky: No.

Gallagher: If I don't bring him in the coyotes might get 'im.

Nicky: *Bad* coyotes.

Gallagher: That bear have a name?

Nicky: Uh-uh. *She stares into creek.* When I was small I almost drowned, you know.

Gallagher: Is that a fact.

Nicky: There was a stream which ran by our house. One day I thought I'd cross to the other side where the big moths with brown wings all lived. But it was deeper than I thought and I slipped on the rocks and went under the water and it was just lucky that the young man who lived next door came along and he saved me. His name was Bobby. He was the fire chief's son. He gave me mouth-to-mouth on the bank of stream. It was the first time I had ever touched a grown man, who wasn't my father, on the lips. When I got older we met up again and we fell in love. Some of this is true, and some of this isn't. You're a smart man. Can you guess which is which?

Gallagher: I guess I'm not that smart.

Nicky: Is your coalmine nearby?

Gallagher: Over there.

Nicky: Show me your dinosaur, will you?

Gallagher: It's pretty late.

Nicky: *Suddenly all grown up.* I'm wide awake.

Lights up briefly on Bobby in the guest room looking out the window towards the creek.

Bobby: I'm way of ahead of you Nicky. Way ahead.

TWENTY-SEVEN

INSIDE GALLAGHER'S MINE

The dinosaur skeleton glares out of the wall of rock. Nicky's in awe of it.

Gallagher: Pretty amazing, huh?

Nicky: How did you not notice it for two years?

Gallagher: Mystery to me.

Nicky: Can I feel it? I'll be gentle.

Gallagher: *Shrugs.* It's made of rock.

Nicky: *Feeling it.* It wasn't *always* made of rock.

Gallagher: Dr. Bloomfield doesn't know what it is. He thinks it might be a new species of some kind.

Nicky: A new species.

Gallagher: Newly discovered he means, by scientists, for the very first time anywhere. Personally I think it was some kind of diabolical storm that killed them all off.

Nicky: Maybe they were just unfit.

Gallagher: What do you mean?

Nicky: Maybe the dinosaurs weren't good enough to live, a mistake of nature, that needed to be done all over again. This one had already started to change. Can you see? It looks like a bird. Can you see that?

Gallagher: Now that you mention it...

Nicky: I have a secret.

Gallagher: I'm glad there's still one left.

Nicky: It's a terrible secret. I'm in a lot of trouble, Mr. Gallagher. We're not on our honeymoon, the man is not my husband. Should I go on?

Gallagher: It's *your* secret.

Nicky: He murdered my mother and father.

Gallagher: That's more than I expected. Are you telling me the truth now?

Nicky: I met him at the bakery and we took a shine to each other.

Gallagher: Go on then. Go slowly.

Nicky: He kept coming back and then one day he asked me out to a party where I learned he'd been in prison and had just been released. He's very charming though and I believed him when he said he'd turned over a new leaf in his life and he got me talking all about *my* life and I confessed to him that my father had been very bad to me when I was young. Then I told him that my father was a superstitious old miser who kept all his money at home in a safe and we decided that we would *steal* my father's money and run away together. My mother was supposed to be in the psychiatric unit of the hospital and my father was supposed to be at work but we were wrong on both counts. My father had taken the day off to bring my mother home for the holiday weekend. The rest is very bloody.

Gallagher: I guess there's no going back now, eh?

Nicky: We went to my house to do the deed but my father caught us in the act with a shotgun. He said, honey girl, how *could* you? And I said, it's easy, daddy, and that's when Bobby got the gun away from him and he shot my father in the belly right in front of me. And then my mother walked into the room and she started to scream and scream and scream and he shot her, too. There was so much blood in the room. On the floor, on the walls, on the ceiling, on us. And the next thing I remember we were driving down a road I didn't know. And after a few hours when my mind started to clear up I asked to be let out but he wouldn't give in to me. And he said he would kill me if I ever tried to leave him. I'm terrified of him. You've been suspicious of us all along, Mr. Gallagher, I know you have. You've been in our room, you've been in our car....

During her speech the dinosaur skeleton below will slowly begin to glow until it is glowing blood-red. Gallagher seems hypnotized by her.

Nicky: Save me from him, sir. I'm pleading with you. My father was miserly and dirty and my mother was out of her skull and I'm glad their both out of my life but I don't want to ride into the sunset with their murderer. Be my soldier. I'll pay you to help me, I know you need the money. I'll do anything. Do you want me? You can have me right here if you like. My name is Nicky. I'm only nineteen years old. Or fifteen...or thirteen...or eleven...or ten... *She lies back for him.*

Gallagher approaches her slowly — straddles her — and strangles her to death. We hear machinegun fire.

Gallagher: Let me be...you can't have me...

TWENTY-EIGHT

GUEST ROOM

Next morning. Hannah comes to the door of the guest room with a breakfast tray.

Hannah: *Knocks.* Hello this room. *Knocks again.* Good morning, you two — it's nearly noon. *She opens the door and looks in.*

Lights up on the bed where only one person lies.

Hannah: Breakfast in bed for the newlyweds.

Nicky sits up.

Nicky: I'm starving.

Hannah: Where's the groom?

Nicky: *Looks beside her.* I don't know.

TWENTY-NINE

THE MOUTH OF GALLAGHER'S MINE

Bobby approaches.

Bobby: Dr. Bloomfield?

Dr. Bloomfield: *Within.* Yes?

Bobby: How's it goin' in there?

Dr. Bloomfield: Fine, thank you. Is that Mr. Snow?

Bobby: Yeh. Can I see you for a minute?

Dr. Bloomfield: Just a second.

A moment, then Dr. Bloomfield comes out of the mineshaft carrying a brush in one hand and an awl in the other. His face and clothes are smudged with dirt and coal dust.

Dr. Bloomfield: Good morning.

Bobby: You look like you just crawled out of your own grave. *They both laugh.* It's noon.

Dr. Bloomfield: Time skitters by when one's communing with the deep past... or words to that effect. *Both laugh again.*

Bobby: How long have you been up?

Dr. Bloomfield: Crack of dawn actually. Hangover and all. How are *you* feeling today?

Bobby: Oh, I've been better.

Dr. Bloomfield: *Laughs.* What can I do for you, Mr. Snow?

Bobby: Well I'm wondering, sir, if I could borrow your car for a little bit. I'd like to drive to Drumheller and check on my repairs. I hate to ask Mr. Gallagher because he's already done so much for us.

Dr. Bloomfield: Oh — well — I don't see why not. I have to be leaving for Edmonton shortly after lunch though...

Bobby: Have'er back in a flash.

Dr. Bloomfield: All right then. Happy to be of help. *Fishes his keys from his pocket and gives them to him.*

Bobby: Grateful. *It thunders.* Might storm.

Dr. Bloomfield: Indeed.

THIRTY

GALLAGHER'S SHACK / PRISON CELL

More thunder. Gallagher is seated on a cot. Every time it thunders bars of light flash around him like a prison cell and he trembles terribly.

Gallagher: *Shouts.* LET ME BE!

A loud blast of thunder — a blinding flash of lightning. We hear the clang of doors...the thunder slowly fades away...and Hannah enters the space.

Hannah: John...? *Gallagher doesn't regard her at all.* I feel awful about what happened last night. I stayed awake for hours, I was hoping you'd come back. *He doesn't respond.* Is there something the matter with you, John? *Goes to him.* God, you look awful.

Gallagher: I had one of my spells, Hannah.

Hannah: *Takes his face in her hands.* Look at me, John.

Gallagher: It was a bad one.

Hannah: Talk it through. Come on.

Gallagher: The dog went missing. I was afraid he might've been chased by coyotes. So I took my gun. Went looking for him. I saw Mrs. Snow by the creek. We went to see my dinosaur. We were talking about...birds, I think...and that's when the spell grabbed onto me and I was suddenly back in the war. And when I came out of it I was walking way up in the hills, the sun was rising, the dog was with me, I couldn't remember *anything*. And then it thundered like bombs falling down. I ran all the way home. Haven't moved from this spot. Can't.

Hannah: You probably haven't slept either. *She starts to take his boots off.* Did you have one of your visions, too?

Gallagher: *Thinks.* Oh yeh... *Little laugh.* ...I imagined my dinosaur came alive and he ate everybody.

Hannah: You're losing credibility, John.

Gallagher: *Laughs again.* Aren't I. *It thunders. He trembles.* They aren't who they say they are, Hannah. They're entirely different people.

Hannah: Who are you talking about?

Gallagher: The newlyweds.

Hannah: I don't understand you.

Gallagher: It's all adding up. Mr. Snow didn't know what a Mountie was, Mrs. Snow didn't know how far away Banff was, and neither of them knew the nickname for Medicine Hat. And Hannah, I found a revolver in Mr. Snow's jacket earlier and a suitcase full of American money. No, they aren't who they say they are, not by a longshot.

Hannah: *Beat.* I see.

Gallagher: They might have a price on their heads, wouldn't that be lucky.

Curt McInstry as John Gallagher and Suzanne McDowell as Hannah Bruce. (Thomas Usher)

Hannah: So what do we do now?

Gallagher: Tomorrow I'll report them to the police in Calgary and see what turns up.

Hannah: They'll likely be gone tomorrow.

Gallagher: I think I fixed it so they won't be.

Hannah: How?

Gallagher: I drove back to Drumheller last night. Started their car up and ran it until it was hot — she'll likely seize overnight without a good cooling system.

Hannah: What if we're wrong?

Gallagher: It's only a Plymouth.

Hannah: You're a hounddog, John.

Gallagher: I feel like a cop again.

Hannah: Well that's a good thing. I won't be too comfortable with unknown people with guns in my house.

Gallagher: You know, Hannah...when the spell grabs on to me...it's like I can feel a cold wind rushing into my brain through that hole in my head...and I see things in there that a man shouldn't normally see.

Hannah: Lie down, my love. Get some sleep. *She helps him.* I'll shout for you if anything important happens. *He closes his eyes. She kisses his cheek.* Oh, John.

THIRTY-ONE

GUEST ROOM

Nicky, still in bed, devours the food from the tray with her hands. The meal is all over her face, on her clothes.

Bobby: Mechanic says the engine's seized up and it might be shot altogether. I told him we'd think about it but as far as I'm concerned it ain't worth fixin'. Good thing we have an option. *Shows keys.* It's a Buick. *Grins.* There's been a change of plans. That mechanic had a magazine in his crapper which had an article about Seattle, Washington in it. They have casinos in Seattle, Washington. They have a big amusement park there and lots of other fun stuff, too. It's closer than Alaska and it don't involve boats or trains. We're going to zoom there in the doctor's nice car and disappear into the scenery.

Nicky: *Pushes the tray away.* You are.

Bobby: What're you talking about?

Nicky: I'm not going with you, I want my half of the money.

Bobby: Well you're not going to get it. We're in this together, we're *bonded*.

Nicky: I want to be *un*bonded.

Bobby: Well you *can't* be.

Nicky: I am *ending* this thing!

Bobby: THIS THING DON'T END! You know that, baby. You know it, kid. It ain't just the money and it ain't just the death. It's *us*. We're connected all up and down our bodies and in our blood and in our very souls. We. Are. Bonded. It's a spiritual bonding without no end. *He kisses her hard on the mouth.* No end. *Beat.* We just need some new names again. *Grins.* Now get yourself dressed.

He exits. She sits motionlessly for a long moment.

THIRTY-TWO

THE MOUTH OF GALLAGHER'S MINE

Bobby: Dr. Bloomfield?

Dr. Bloomfield: *Within.* Yes?

Bobby: I've brung your car keys back. *Jingles them.*

Dr. Bloomfield: I'll be right out.

Bobby: That's okay, I'll come in. *If* you don't mind. *He draws his gun, glances over his shoulder, and disappears into the mineshaft.*

Dr. Bloomfield: Watch out for that light stand, it's a little bit —

Black out.

THIRTY-THREE

GALLAGHER'S SHACK

Gallagher sleeps. A knock at the door, then Nicky enters with a suitcase.

Nicky: Mr. Gallagher? Are you resting?

Hannah approaches the mineshaft.

Hannah: Dr. Bloomfield?

Nicky: It's me.

THIRTY-FOUR

THE MOUTH OF GALLAGHER'S MINE

Hannah: I've made some lunch for you. *Beat.* Are you in there, Doctor? *She starts to go in and comes face to face with Bobby coming out.*

Hannah: Oh! Scared me.

Bobby: The doctor's not in there.

Hannah: Are you sure?

Bobby: I brought his keys back, I'd borrowed his car to drive into Drumheller. Check on our repairs. He's not in there at all.

Hannah: What did you learn about your car?

Bobby: There's been some heat damage. I was hoping to find Mr. Gallagher and ask for his advice. Since he knows about cars. Is that his shack over there?

Hannah: *Hesitates.* Yes.

Bobby: His car's there.

Hannah: I was just over there, he's gone on foot somewhere.

Bobby: Maybe they've gone off together...he and the doctor.

Hannah: Maybe they walked into Carbon to the hardware store for something.

Bobby: That sounds possible.

Hannah: A light bulb or something.

Bobby: Some kind of fixture, a fuse, a tool...

Hannah: That's likely.

Bobby: I'll walk with you back to the house.

Hannah: You go ahead. There's an old coalminer who lives down the creek a ways. He's been sick, I promised to look in on him.

Bobby: You're a very kind woman, Miss Bruce.

Hannah: It's a small community, we all — *Mr. Snow draws his gun.*

Bobby: Get inside there.

Hannah: *Shouts.* John! *He clubs her with his gun — she falls. He drags her into the shaft. A loud crack of thunder and lightning.*

THIRTY-FIVE

GALLAGHER'S SHACK AND SURROUNDING AREA

Nicky is seated on Gallagher's cot. Gallagher stands staring out the window. Thunder.

Nicky: We're alike you and I. We're both damaged goods, we both want a new lease on life. I want to run away with you, Mr. Gallagher. Is that so shocking? I don't think so. What's holding you here? That fucking hole in the side of a hill? I don't think so. Miss Bruce? You don't love her. Tell me you do. You don't, you can't. It's a lot of cash, Mr. Gallagher. His whole life savings. My father was the firechief.

Gallagher: Good for him.

Nicky: Didn't last night mean *anything* to you?

Gallagher: I don't remember last night.

Nicky: I could remind you.

Gallagher: I don't doubt that you could.

Nicky: He'll find me here, Mr. Gallagher. It's only a matter of time, he'll put us together. He has a gun and he's crazy.

Gallagher: I've known a lot crazier.

Nicky: You're not the least bit afraid of him are you.

Gallagher: Does he love you?

Nicky: Can murderers really love? *Pause.*

Gallagher: I had a vision of you last night. You and me. I dreamed that I brutalized you with my own bare hands. Left you in the coalmine to rot. Am I really the one you want to run away with then?

Nicky: *Smiles.* Such a strange, strange man.

Lights up on the mouth Gallagher's mine: Bobby sticks his head out, gun in hand, wearing the doctor's hat and glasses. Gallagher sees him through his window.

Gallagher: What the hell...?

Nicky: What is it?

Gallagher: It's the doctor. He's in my mineshaft. He has a gun. Just a second...

Bobby can barely keep from laughing now. He looks half-crazed.

Bobby: Gallagher!

Gallagher: What do you want, Mr. Snow?

Nicky: *Rises.* Is it him?

Bobby: You know what I want. I know she's over there. Nicky!

Nicky: I'm not going with you!

Bobby: You come out here!

Nicky: I've told him everything, Bobby!

Bobby: I've got Miss Bruce and the doctor over here, Gallagher. They're inside your mine here. They ain't hurt yet but they will be. I'll kill them both without compunction. Not a smidgen. Then I'll come over there and I'll kill you, too. I'm a killer, son. Natural and born. They'll be talking about me way into the future.

Nicky: You don't have the nerve!

Bobby: You know I do!

Nicky: This man was in the *war*!

Bobby: I don't care!

Nicky: I hate you!

Bobby: I know you don't!

Gallagher: I want to see them, Mr. Snow. Bring them out here.

Nicky: I *despise* you!

Gallagher: *To her.* Shut *up* for a second.

Bobby: Do you think I already killed them, Gallagher?

Gallagher: I have to know.

Bobby: I might've. It's in my nature. Killers like me have virtually no compunction. You used to be a policeman, you know the likes of me. I'm cold to the bone. Make Nicky come out here!

Gallagher: Show me the hostages first!

Bobby: *You* go first!

Gallagher: *To Nicky.* We're in a kind of stalemate here.

Nicky: Naw, he's just shooting off at the mouth, I've seen him like this before, he's brave with a gun. Don't *you* have a gun by the way?

Gallagher: Well I do but I lost it somewhere last night.

Nicky: Welcome to Canada. Where I come from everyone would be blasting away by now.

Gallagher: He *thinks* I have one and that's what counts.

Bobby: Gallagher!

Gallagher: What?

Bobby: Well I'm waiting!

Gallagher: So am I!

Bobby: I'm going to count to three and then I'm gonna kill them. Did you hear me, Gallagher?

Gallagher: I hear ya.

Bobby: You know I'm serious then.

Gallagher: You'll be sure to count loudly then.

Bobby: Damn rights I will.

Gallagher: Okay.

Bobby: ONE!

Nicky: What're you going to do?

Gallagher: I'm going to set fire to my shack.

Nicky: I beg your pardon.

Bobby: TWO!

Gallagher: It'll go up in a flash, and it's been a dry summer, it'll spread like crazy. *As he starts spreading fuel around.*

Bobby: Do hear me counting, Gallagher?!

Gallagher: We'll escape in the smoke. You take the suitcase and go down to the creek, you'll be safe there. I wager he'll panic and I'll look for my chance.

Bobby: *Gallagher!*

Gallagher: Get ready. *He lights a match…*

Fire and smoke! Nicky runs toward the creek. Bobby sees her and goes after her but Gallagher intercepts him. They fight for the gun, it's flung to the ground, and Gallagher easily subdues him. Nicky approaches with a suitcase. She sees the gun and picks it up. Points it.

Nicky: Get off him, Mr. Gallagher.

Gallagher: Give me the gun.

Bobby: Shoot him, Nicky.

Nicky: Move away from him! *He does. She turns the gun on Bobby.*

Bobby: Don't do anything stupid, kid. We're home free now. Let's just skidaddle.

Nicky: I don't want to skidaddle.

Bobby: What do you *want* then?

Nicky: I want my whole life back.

Bobby: It's history now!

Nicky: I deny it!

Bobby: You CAN'T deny it!

Nicky: But I *DO!*

Bobby: Explain that to me, I must be stupid.

Nicky: If a person *says* something didn't happen and goes on *living* like it didn't happen, then for all intents and purposes it may as well not even have happened at *all*. It's a trick of the mind a person can do.

Bobby: That's way over my head, baby.

Gallagher: Give me the gun.

Nicky: No! *She turns it back on Gallagher.*

Bobby: I love you, kid.

Nicky: Murderers can't be lovers.

Bobby: *Any*body can be lovers. You *know* that, honey girl. We are the living PROOF of that.

Nicky: I want to fly free like a bird! *Turns the gun on Bobby.*

Bobby: Look in the suitcase.

Nicky: Why?

Bobby: It's proof of how much I love you. Open it up. Go *on!*

She dumps it on the ground — no money. I was awake last night when you left our bed and went out. I watched you out the window walking by the creek with your teddy bear and I saw you meet up with him. What'd she tell ya, Gallagher? Did she cry and flutter her eyeballs at you? I've seen her do that her whole blamed life.

Gallagher: Give me the gun, Nicky. *She aims at Gallagher again.*

Bobby: I could've zoomed off in the doctor's nice car and left you high and dry — *but I didn't!* And that's because we're bonded. You can do it now, kid. Just squeeze the trigger.

Nicky: Where's the money?

Bobby: It's in a safe place.

Nicky: *Back on Bobby.* I'll kill you, Bobby.

Bobby: No you won't.

Nicky: I *will!*

Bobby: You can't live without me, girl.

Nicky: I want to die and be born again differently.

She points it at her own head.

Bobby: Don't do it, kid.

Gallagher lunges and grabs her from behind. He takes hold of her wrist and draws the gun away from her head. He whispers in her ear.

Gallagher: You don't have to die to be born again, Nicky. *And he trains the gun still in Nicky's hand onto Bobby.*

Bobby: Jeez, Nicky.

Black out...silence...then a loud explosion.

THIRTY-SIX

HANNAH'S SITTING ROOM

Rain on the roof. Hannah sits alone with a cold compress on the side of her head. Dr. Bloomfield enters slowly from off. He has a compress, too. They both look awful.

Dr. Bloomfield: I'm claustrophobic, you know.

Hannah: Have some more moonshine.

Dr. Bloomfield: I don't understand what's happened. Where did Mr. Gallagher go after he freed us from the mineshaft? Where are the newlyweds? What was that explosion?

Hannah: Don't excite yourself, Doctor.

Dr. Bloomfield: He took my wallet, my glasses...!

Hannah: You survived it.

Dr. Bloomfield: He put a pistol to my head!

Hannah: Have some more moonshine.

Gallagher enters.

Dr. Bloomfield: Mr. Gallagher!

Gallagher: Everyone doin' all right?

Hannah: We're getting there.

Dr. Bloomfield: What was that explosion?

Gallagher: Dynamite. Had a stick in the mouth of my mineshaft. Fire spread to it.

Dr. Bloomfield: *Clutches his chest.* Good God!

Hannah: Where are the newlyweds, John?

Gallagher: They stole my car. They've gone. And they weren't even newlyweds...far from it, I think.

Dr. Bloomfield: Liars and thieves!

Hannah: What were they, love?

Gallagher: They were children, love. *They exchange a knowing look.*

Dr. Bloomfield: *Still beside himself.* How do people *get* like that?

Gallagher: Weak moral fibre?

Hannah: Bad upbringing? *Both laugh a little.*

Dr. Bloomfield: And the dinosaur...?

Gallagher: There's always another one, Doc. Bloomin' hills are full of 'em.

Sound of sirens.

Hannah: Drumheller firebrigade.

Gallagher: Little late I'd say.

Dr. Bloomfield: I want to go home.

THIRTY-SEVEN

HANNAH'S FRONT STEPS

Days later. Hannah sits alone on the steps with a glass of lemonade, staring into space. Now Nicky approaches from off with a basket full of wild flowers. She sits beside Hannah.

Lights up on the Old Woman looking on from the present.

Hannah: Arson.

Nicky and Old Woman: How long did he get?

Hannah: Ten years.

Nicky: Seems pretty steep for the crime.

Hannah: Same judge who tried him for killing John Coward. Did I miss anything while I was gone?

Nicky: Man came by for some moonshine. He gave me the money, I gave him a bottle, he didn't even bat an eye. I could've been you.

Hannah: I've been faceless in this town since the day I arrived.

Nicky: Is that why you like it here?

Hannah: Maybe.

Nicky: I like it here. It's grown on me. Oh yeh, something else. I went for a walk with Mr. Gallagher's dog way up in the hills just now and I found something which I think might belong to him. *She reveals a revolver from the basket.*

Hannah: That's his all right. *She takes it. Looks at it. Pause.*

Nicky: Do you think Mr. Gallagher knows where my father's money is, Hannah?

Hannah: He hasn't said he does.

Nicky: And you don't either, huh? Is that honest?

Hannah: You've seen me, girl, I've turned the whole house upside-down.

Nicky: Maybe it got burned up.

Hannah: It might've.

Silence.

Nicky: I do like it here though. It's a mysterious type of land which really does grow on you. *Hannah turns and gazes at her.*

Old Woman: Even the creatures do.

Nicky: Even the creatures do.

THIRTY-EIGHT

PRISON CELL

Gallagher is seated on a cot in prison clothes. The clang of doors and Hannah enters the cell with a brown paper bag. She sits beside him. A moment...

Hannah: Nicky tried to kill herself a few days ago. She tied a noose in the rope of the swing set. I just happened to look out the window.

Gallagher: She's a troubled young woman.

Hannah: She is.

Gallagher: How's my dog?

Hannah: He's fine. He's taken to Nicky quite well actually. They go walking in the hills together now.

Gallagher: How nice.

Hannah: How's the food in here?

Gallagher: Not very good.

Hannah: I brought some homecooking.

Gallagher: Thank you. *Opens bag and starts to sample the food.*

Hannah: That mechanic from Drumheller came by the house. He wanted me to ask you what he should do with that Plymouth he still has on his premises.

Gallagher: Tell him to tear it down and use it for parts.

Hannah: All right. *Pause.* I got a letter from Dr. Bloomfield. He said to say hello.

Gallagher: Hello.

Hannah: He's going back to London, England to work with a team of paleontologists from all around the world. It's a real big deal. They're trying to raise money to go to China to dig for bones. Apparently there were some dinosaurs over there in the Gobi Desert which make ours look small. Oh yeh, and somebody from Ottawa is talking about setting up a little museum down in Steveville. I read it in the paper.

Gallagher: That was my idea.

Hannah: The doctor inquired about his journal, too. Seems he misplaced it and he thought he might've left it at the house somewhere.

Gallagher: Did you find it?

Hannah: No. He has a photographic memory though, he can write it all down again if he wants to.

Gallagher: This is a good meatloaf, Hannah.

Hannah: Have you had any spells in here?

Gallagher: *Shakes his head.* No.

Hannah: Though I bet if you had one you'd get some attention, huh? It might get you moved to different quarters. Might be an opportunity there. In that. You know, getting moved. Might be worth even faking one.

Gallagher: I don't know how to fake one.

Hannah: Foam at the mouth.

Gallagher: Isn't dignified.

Hannah: John, I've been missing you so much I can hardly sleep at night, I mean it.

Gallagher: I miss you, too.

Hannah: I'll go crazy in ten years, *I'll* kill myself.

Gallagher: Don't talk like that.

Hannah: Would you do something, John? Would you reach up my dress and remind me of your touch?

Gallagher: *Looks at her.* Right now?

Hannah: Please, John. Reach up my dress and touch me. Nobody will see. *He does.* That's it. Keep going. Little further...

Gallagher pulls his hand back out — with a gun in it — which he quickly hides.

Hannah: I believe you know where the money is, love.

Gallagher: Do you now?

Hannah: I do. *She puts her hand on his leg. Pause.*

Gallagher: Foam at the mouth, eh?

She smiles.

THIRTY-NINE

VISION QUEST SITE IN THE PRESENT

The skull sits between them.

Frank Bloomfield: After you gave the pistol to Gallagher did you ever see him again?

Old Woman: No.

Frank Bloomfield: He knew where the money was hidden?

Old Woman: I believe Mr. Snow had stashed the money in the trunk of your grandfather's car. John must have figured that out somehow and after he blew up his mine on top of Mr. Snow's body he buried the money in the trees behind the house. And after he escaped from prison he came back and dug it up...the money.

Frank Bloomfield: How do you know?

Old Woman: I found the hole.

Frank Bloomfield: Ah.

Old Woman: I'd been called to Drumheller to see the police and when I got home his dog was gone and so was Nicky.

Frank Bloomfield: They'd run off together.

Old Woman: I believe so, yes.

Frank Bloomfield: That must have been hard for you.

Old Woman: I stayed with the land — it's dependable.

Frank Bloomfield: *Picks up the skull.* And you, Miss Bruce, what happened next for you? When did you give up the bed-and-breakfast?

Old Woman: Soon after. It wasn't profitable. I sold the house to a man from Drumheller and I moved to Steveville, then Brooks, then Medicine Hat where you found me. I had various jobs in the food industry over the years and I've travelled a fair bit.

Frank Bloomfield: Amazing story.

Old Woman: You said you never knew your grandfather. What happened to him finally?

Frank Bloomfield: Oh, he was caught in an avalanche while digging for bones in China. When they got to him he was still alive. He'd been there, swallowed up by the earth, for three whole days. Died shortly thereafter.

Old Woman: He had claustrophobia.

Frank Bloomfield: Yeh I know.

Old Woman: Do *you*?

Frank Bloomfield: No, I'm afraid of heights. What about you? Any old fears?

Old Woman: I'm a bit nervous around water to tell the truth.
I nearly drowned when I was small. My brother saved me.
He went on to be a lifeguard, you know.

Frank Bloomfield: I thought you were left on the steps of a...
A sudden realization: he gazes at her.

Old Woman: Sun's going down.

Frank Bloomfield: *Smiles to himself.* Yes.

Old Woman: Did you get everything from me for your book you
were hoping for, Mr. Bloomfield?

Frank Bloomfield: I think so, yes. *Puts his finger in bullet hole.*

Old Woman: Look! There's a nightowl. Beautiful birds.
Mysterious cry they make.

Frank Bloomfield: *Nods.* Yes.

*Lights up slowly on Hannah's backyard where Nicky, wearing
Hannah's clothes, is hanging laundry in the sunshine. She gazes out
over the land now...*

...as Frank Bloomfield approaches the audience.

Frank Bloomfield: When travelling through the badlands of North
America a person must use caution. One: Make sure all of
your gauges are working properly. Two: Carry extra fuel and
water. Three: Be wary of rattlesnakes and scorpions. Four:
Respect the fragility of cliff embankments, hoodoos, gorges,
and ancient Aboriginal rock formations. Five: Don't open
your door to strangers unless they are in obvious trouble
for having failed in one or more of the above said-cautions.
And have a good trip — it may be your last.

*Images of the badlands are superimposed all over the stage...and fade
to black.*

END

Gordon Pengilly was raised on a farm near Lethbridge, Alberta and currently lives in Calgary. From 1971-78 he studied at the University of Alberta, earning a BA in Drama and an MFA in Playwriting, the first graduate of that degree. A versatile writer, Pengilly has written more than fifty plays for television, film, radio, and the stage.

Pengilly's awards include the Writers Guild of Canada Jim Burt Screenwriting Prize for *Drumheller or Dangerous Times*, the BBC International Radio Drama Prize for *Seeing in the Dark*, and many provincial and national awards, most notably the 75th Anniversary Walterdale Theatre Award for *The Apprentice of Swipe*, the Edmonton Journal Award for *Seeds*, and several Alberta Playwriting Competition first place prizes for *Metastasis, Seeds, Brawler Takes the Count*, and *The Whole Distance*. He has also been a finalist in the Ottawa Little Theatre Competition for *Seeds*, the Herman Voaden National Competition for *Metastasis*, the du Maurier National for *Tom Form and the Speed of Love*, the Neptune Theatre Trident National for *Harm's Way*, and the Scriptapalooza Hollywood Screenplay Contest for *Harm's Way*. Co-written with Theatre Network, *Hardhats and Stolen Hearts* was one of the first Canadian plays performed off-Broadway at the Performance Garage in 1978.

Pengilly has worked on two children's television series and three documentaries. He has also read feature film scripts for the A-Channel Drama Fund. One of Canada's most prolific radio dramatists, his plays have been aired in the United States, Australia, and on the BBC World Service. Also a published poet, he is a past poetry editor for *Dandelion Magazine* and has taught scriptwriting at Mount Royal College. Pengilly has been resident playwright for theatres and institutions in Edmonton, Calgary, Red Deer, Banff, Toronto, and Fredericton. He routinely runs workshops for Alberta Playwrights Network and has been associated with CAPES (Calgary Arts Partners in Education Society) for several years. His newest play, *Flesh and Ghost*, is being developed by Theatre Calgary.

COMPLETE PLAYLIST

STAGE PLAYS (PREMIERES)

Peck the Woodstick. U of A Drama Department, Edmonton. 1975. Dir. Audie Lew

Brawler Takes the Count. U of A Drama Department, Edmonton. 1976. Dir. Lewis Evans

Seeds. U of A Drama Department, Edmonton. 1977. Dir. Keith Digby

Hard Hats and Stolen Hearts (co-written with Theatre Network). Theatre 3, Edmonton. 1977. Dir. Mark Manson

Kicker (co-written with Theatre Network). Theatre 3, Edmonton. 1978. Dir. Mark Manson

Songs for Believers. U of A, Studio Theatre, Edmonton. 1978. Dir. Frank Buekert

Flibbertygibbet (music: Jan Randall). Workshop West, Edmonton. 1979. Dir. Stephen Heatley

Kootenai (music: Jan Randall). Cardston Community Theatre. 1980. Dir. Terry Petrie

The Apprentice of Swipe. Walterdale Theatre, Edmonton. 1981. Dir. Larry Farley

Swipe. NDWT Theatre Company / Toronto Free Theatre. 1982. Dir. Keith Turnbull

Alice on Stage (music: Jan Randall). Theatre Calgary. 1985. Dir. John Palmer

Lucky Girl (music: Ron Dann). Red Deer College. 1989. Dir. Larry Reese

God's Dice (music: Jonathan Dean). Banff Centre for the Arts. 1989. Dir. John Paul Fischbach

Yours 'Til the Moon Falls Down (music: Tim Williams). Lunchbox Theatre, Calgary. 1992. Dir. Tom Kerr

They Don't Call Them Farmers Anymore. Alberta Repertoire

Theatre, Lethbridge. 1993. Dir. David McNary

Metastasis. Northern Light Theatre, Edmonton. 1995. Dir. DD Kugler

The Saga of Tom Three Persons. Prime Stock / Empress Theatre, Fort Macleod. 1996. Dir. Thomas Usher

Wildcat! (music: Ron Casat). Prime Stock Theatre, Turner Valley. 1999. Dir. Thomas Usher

Fool's Paradise. Empress Theatre, Fort Macleod. 2000. Dir. Thomas Usher

Drumheller or Dangerous Times. Prime Stock Theatre, Red Deer. 2001. Dir. Thomas Usher

Contraption. Jagged Edge Theatre, Edmonton. 2002. Dir. Amy DeFelice

The Work Play. Actor's Loft, New York. 2003. Dir. Joseph Andorfer

The Ballad of an Existential Cowboy. F.R.H. Drama, Festival Place, Edmonton. 2006. Dir. Monty Drozda

Tom Form (music: Victor Bateman). New Theatre Projects / Theatre Passe Muraille, Toronto. 2006. Dir. Bill Lane

Love / Talk. Image Theatre, "Imagepalooza", Edmonton. 2006. Dir. Dave Owen

PLAYS IN DEVELOPMENT

Look Back Time. Alberta Foundation for the Arts / Alberta Playwrights Network.

Flesh and Ghost. Theatre Calgary.

RADIO PLAYS

Seeds. CBC Stage, Edmonton. 1978. Dir. Mark Schoenberg

The Vidocq Society (co-written with Ben Tarver). CBC Playhouse, Winnipeg. 1979. Dir. Colin Jackson

Lucky Girl. CBC Vanishing Point, Toronto. 1986. Dir. Bill Lane

The Rawhide Hour. CBC Vanishing Point, Edmonton. 1987. Dir. Mark Schoenberg

The Ballad of an Existential Cowboy. CBC Vanishing Point, Calgary. 1989. Dir. Martie Fishman

The Conscription Stand-off of 1918. Access-CKUA, Edmonton. 1989. Dir. Colin McLean

The Carbon Murders. Access-CKUA, Edmonton. 1990. Dir. Colin McLean

The Black Candle. Access-CKUA, Edmonton. 1990. Dir. Colin McLean

The Saga of Tom Three Persons. (Five episodes) CBC Morningside, Calgary. 1990. Dir. Martie Fishman

The Cow Poems. CBC Anthology, Edmonton. 1990.

The Old Man's Rock. CBC Carte Blanche, Calgary. 1992. Dir. Martie Fishman

They Don't Call Them Farmers Anymore. CBC Carte Blanche, Calgary. 1992. Dir. Martie Fishman

In the Middle of Town Stands the Dreamland. CBC Stereodrama, Calgary. 1993. Dir. Martie Fishman

Looking for Red. CBC Stereodrama, Calgary. 1995. Dir. Martie Fishman

An Audible Feast. Live from Heritage Park, CBC Calgary. 1995. Dir. Martie Fishman

Tom Form and the Speed of Love. CBC Studio 96, Toronto. 1996. Dir. Bill Lane

The Cormorant. CBC Sunday Showcase, Calgary. 1997. Dir. Martie Fishman

Bailey's Way. (Thirteen episodes) The Mystery Project, CBC Calgary. 1998 – 1999. Dir. Martie Fishman

The Boat (from the short story by Alistair Macleod). CBC Summer Festival, Toronto. 2002. Dir. Bill Lane

Seeing in the Dark. BBC World Drama, London, UK. 2007. Dir. Anne Edyvean

TELEVISION / VIDEO

Seeds. Cable 10, Edmonton. 1978. Dir. Keith Digby

Nuggets. (Three episodes) ITV, Edmonton. 1979. Prod. Steven Best

The Magic Ring. (Four episodes) Access/CKUA-TV, Calgary. 1980. Dir. Gene Packwood

Voices in the Wind. White Iron Film & Video, Calgary, for Martel Enterprises, Germany. 1992. Dir. Vern Braun

SHORT FILMS

Work / Play. Early Next Week Productions, Los Angeles, CA. Shown at Fourth Wall Screenings, Hollywood, CA. 2005. Dir. Devon Michaels & Stan Klimecko

SCREENPLAYS IN DEVELOPMENT

Looking for Red. Developed by Telefilm Canada Cross-over Writer's Program, Vancouver.

Drumheller or Dangerous Times. Developed by Praxis Centre of Screenwriters, Vancouver.

Harm's Way. Developed at Praxis Centre for Screenwriters, Vancouver.